D1370516

No Port in a Storm

No Port in a Storm

Bob MacAlindin

WHITTLES PUBLISHING

Frontis

A common enough occurrence in the days of sail, depicted here in Boy's Own Paper. Part of the reason for the staggering number of shipwrecks was unseaworthy ships and trust to luck navigation. Lightships played a crucial role in making the seas safer for mariners. Their most valuable work in terms of lives saved was done in the 19th century when their widespread disposition coincided with crude and sometimes non-existent navigation techniques aboard sailing vessels.

Published by:
Whittles Publishing
Roseleigh House, Latheronwheel. Caithness, KW5 6DW, Scotland.

ISBN 1-870325-37-0

Designed by Janet Watson

Printed by Interprint Ltd., Malta

Contents

Introduction   ix
The Nantucket Lightship Station   1
LV XX (Vyl)   12
LS 83 (Blunt's Reef)   19
LV Comet (Daunt Rock)   25
LV Manicouagan   33
LV 61 (East Dudgeon)   36
LV North Carr   41
The *Channel Rock* Lightship   55
The *Falls* Lightship   69
LV Pharos   73
LV 90 (South Goodwin)   83
LS 82 (Buffalo)   91
LV Storbrotten   95
BF 7 (Ruytingen 1938)   99
LV 19 (Halifax)   101
The Newarp Lightship Station   107
LS 50 (Columbia River)   111
LV 38 (Gull, Brake)   115
Reading Lights   121
The *Abertay* Lightship (1877-1939)   126
Lightships of the Yangtze River   139
Bibliography and source notes   145

Preface

*I*n the course of researching material for this book about lightships it has been my good fortune to make friends of strangers, often in far-off lands. It has not been a grind but a labour of love, enriched by the people who have passed through it and remain within it, giving unstintingly of their time and effort.

I like to think part of the reason for the enthusiasm they have never failed to show is the main reason the book has appeared in the first place – a sense of astonishment that what ought to be so rich a part of the maritime heritage of so many lands flanked by the furious seas has been neglected to the point where the mention of the word 'lightship' is still a good bet to draw the most vacant of looks.

History has dealt harshly with the lightships and those who manned them. There have been few publications about them and here and there in books about lighthouses a chapter or two on lightships might appear. It's almost as though it has been deemed best to draw a veil over the 250 year span of these most expensive of all navigation aids. A case of 'good riddance' perhaps?

I thank all those who have helped me get to the point where I can dare to call this too-slender volume a tribute to lightships and to the people who served upon them with such quiet fortitude. To the forgotten heroes of the bobbing red beacons these chapters are respectfully dedicated.

The *North Carr* lantern delivers a blinding flash. However, this is solar power, not part of the electric system used to power her light. This photograph was taken as the last rays of a winter sunset struck the lantern. The ship was then moored in the outer harbour at Anstruther, Fife where she spent many years as a tourist attraction and museum ship. Photograph, Colin Topping.

Introduction

*T*hink of a ship and the imagery of adventure floods the mind. A destroyer, the greyhound of the ocean, carving through a flat calm, stern dug well in, whirling brass screws transforming water of impossible blue to agitated white. A lifeboat reaching out through the storm to pluck from the jaws of death those in peril on the sea. A graceful tea clipper with a bone in her teeth straining under every stitch of canvas she can carry on the long run home.

The ships of this book – lightships – evoke none of these essentially romantic images. Yet they may be the noblest of them all. Odd creations without doubt were these floating lighthouses, almost always painted a gaudy red – the better to stand out against the blue or grey of the sea – and their names in five foot white letters on each flank. No other ships spent more time at sea, none sailed fewer miles. Their crews, compelled to scan the same lump of water, the same stretch of coastline for the bulk of their working lives, reluctantly lived out the unofficial slogan of the profession: 'Join the service and see the world go by.'

The men strode the decks of stout craft. They had to be. Nature in her foulest moods prompts the prudent seaman to head for the nearest harbour or hasten under the lee of a convenient island. But a forecast of heavy weather for lightshipmen meant making all secure, crossing a finger or two and waiting for the worst. Every once in a while the worst was too much.

What happened to the German lightship *Elbe 1* off the mouth of the River Elbe at 1.40 pm on Wednesday, October 28th, 1936 provides a sombre example. During a north-westerly gale, before the horrified eyes of the captain of the British 1000-ton steamer *The President*, the lightship was hit by a freak wave. Before anyone had time to react she was gone, taking all 15 hands with her. The imagination recoils from the plight of the men trapped in the hull as *Elbe 1* made her tortured, twisting descent to the seabed 80 feet below.

Unlike his colleague the lighthouse keeper, snug in his tower on those nights when the world about him went wild, the life of the lightshipman in a hurricane was a sleepless nightmare of holding on, body braced against every combination of rolling and pitching. Aching muscles laboured ceaselessly to stave off the serious injury that was always a split second away. Tons of water buried the ship as a matter of routine and forced its way inside through the tiniest of cracks, even squirting through keyholes like the jet from a water pistol. And at the back of every man's mind, the fear that the mooring might fail.

Even in less trying conditions, the action of these stumpy ships could be infuriating. A vessel under way delivers a degree of stability in how she reacts to wind and sea. A lightship at anchor is a cork in the water. Her bow rising to meet a wave frequently cannot complete the act, the cable checking her with a shudder that shakes the whole ship.

Little wonder that C. Tucker was moved to write:

> *When a sailor gets to thinking*
> *He is one of the best*
> *Let him ship out on a lightship*
> *And take the acid test*
> *If he still feels like bragging*
> *I don't think that all his tales*
> *Will be of deep sea sailing*
> *But of the ship that never sails*

Danger was a constant shipmate, for foul weather was not the only enemy. Positioned in busy waters, by their presence alone shepherding shipping around reef or sandbank, they could do little to escape the incompetence of others. Occasionally there would be enough time to wind in the cable or let it out, so altering their position to avoid an oncoming vessel but lightships were rammed so often that they carried collision mats to stem the flow of water through damaged hulls.

In wartime, much was added to the customary hazards. Then man, adding to an untold range of reasons for mocking the word civilised, presented himself as an eager seeker of soft targets and lightships were frequently attacked without warning.

The day of the manned lightship is over, one more victim of our demented dash towards a horizon shrouded in the barely understood mists of new technology, littering our wake as we do so with the flotsam of ruined, redundant lives. Those few lightships which still do a job of sorts are fully automated, robots dancing on the sea to a tune orchestrated from the shore, the brainwork behind the system oblivious to the fundamental absurdity of replacing with a few clever toys that living, breathing unit whose capabilities outshine them all by a celestial distance.

As the representative of what is in simple terms a life-saving organisation, today's lightship must stare blankly upon a scene which a few short years ago would have inspired an urgent radio message, or a cool decision, the hurried clump of sea boots along the deck, the lowering of a boat, the reaching out of a helping hand to someone in the direst need of it.

The last manned lightship in the western hemisphere was withdrawn from Belgian waters in February 1994. At most there are two left worldwide, a Russian ship, the *Astrakhanskiy* in the Caspian Sea and one off the coast of Tunisia. By the time these words are read, they too may have gone. The heyday of the lightship was in the early 1900s. More than 750 operated worldwide, employing about 10,000 men and the occasional stewardess.

Already, the people who served on the lightships are forgotten, if indeed their unglamorous way of life was known of at all. Who can guess at the number of lives saved by the service since its stuttering start aboard a converted sloop on the River Thames in 1732? There can be no list of the rescued such as you may find for lifeboat stations. Yet, if prevention really is better than cure, the job done by the lightshipman was the more important. Perhaps for those who survive with only the memory of a thankless job well done, it is enough to know that many a babe opened its eyes on our world because sometime, somewhere, a blazing light on the water steered their forebears away from certain destruction.

In recounting in these pages just a few of the dramas which pepper the history of lightships, the reader may get to know something of the debt owed by the unknowing benefactors of a singular, perilous vocation.

LIGHT BITES

Lightship life was not all drama. Boredom was built into the job. The unusual was therefore welcome, the bizarre a shot in the arm, the downright funny something to be treasured, kept close and savoured time and time again. Many incidents which fall into these categories are unrecorded, lost in a sea of fogged and forgotten memories. But a few survive both the years and the occasionally embroidered telling and are well worth sharing. They are part of the legend of the lightship service. Throughout the book a number of incidents and short tales are recounted as *Light Bites*.

The *South Shoal* Lightship. *Century Magazine*, August, 1891.

The Nantucket
Lightship Station

'The loneliest thing I ever saw,' mused the old whaling skipper, 'was a polar bear on an ice floe. The second loneliest was the *South Shoal* Lightship.'

This solitary sentinel first stood guard over the Nantucket shoals on America's north-eastern seaboard on June 15th, 1854 bearing the ponderous insignia 'Nantucket No 1 New South Shoal.' It was considered the most dangerous and one of the most isolated lightship stations in the world.

Anchored 24 miles off Sankaty Head, Nantucket Island, the ship, LS 11, was specially built for the job at a cost of $3000. She lasted just seven months there before a storm snapped her cable and drove her ashore at Montauk Point, Long Island. Her replacement, LS 1, became a veteran of the station. The station itself was to become something of a nautical nomad, shifting ever further south and south-east. There were two reasons for this.

Firstly, the tides and rips running through and around the shoals made for extreme difficulty in keeping the lightship in one particular place. Up to 1891 LS 1 parted her cable 23 times. The ship was finally withdrawn from service – although not always at Nantucket – in 1930 so it seems fair to assume, even allowing for constant improvements to mooring systems, that she was adrift between 30 and 35 times during her working life. The sum of the fear endured by her crews on such occasions can only be wondered at. In common with most of the lightship service, LS 1 used mushroom-shaped anchors. Today, a crab scuttling along the seabed 190 feet below the position of the long-gone lightship would find itself clanking through a veritable plantation of iron mushrooms.

The second reason lay in the changing character of the shallows, much of which in the mid 19th century remained to be discovered. As later chartwork parted the waters to reveal more and more of Nature's murderous minefield off the Massachusetts coast, the ship had to move accordingly.

The last generation of lightships to serve the area were 47 miles SSE of Nantucket Island, marking the southern limit of the shoals and the eastern end of the Ambrose shipping channel to New York. It is impossible to exaggerate the importance of the ship's presence. Due to the never-ending stream of traffic passing by, including the great passenger liners en route from Europe, this sector was often referred to as 'the Times Square of the North Atlantic'.

By the time the last manned lightship in American waters, no. 612, was withdrawn from this station in 1983, 11 different vessels had served there, not including reliefs. What the ship truly meant to the vessels venturing onto its range was never better captured than by Gustav Kobbé, writing for the August 1891 edition of *Century Magazine* after a spell aboard LS 1. Kobbé's account of life aboard the lightship included the following passage:

> *Through the haze a large three-masted schooner was discernible, heading directly to a reef southwest of us. She was evidently looking for the lightship but the haze had prevented her from sighting us, although our sharp lookout had had his glass on her for some time. Suddenly there was evidence that she had sighted us. She swung around as swiftly as though turning on a pivot. She had been lunging about in a most uncertain way but the sight of us seemed to fill her with new life and buoyancy. Her sails filled, she dashed through the waves with streaks of white streaming along each quarter like foam on the flanks of a race-horse and on she came, fairly quivering with joy from keel to pennant. Such instances occur almost daily and if we add to them the occasions – and they must run into hundreds if not thousands – when the warning voice of the fog bell and the guiding gleam of the lamps have saved vessels from shipwreck, it seems as though the sailor must look upon the South Shoal Lightship as one of the guardian angels of the deep.*

Assuming the mantle of a guardian angel had its drawbacks. With relief trips suspended from December until May, the sight for the crew of the black, side-wheel relief vessel *Verbena* leaving them in December must have been the worst moment of the year, the next chapter of their lives opening slowly before them, each page another endless day upon the icy ocean. Surprisingly, pages which usually remained unturned by the men inhabiting this confined community were those of the books in the tiny library supplied by their employers.

Winters could be unbelievably hard and the 275-ton double-skinned ship needed all her legendary oak toughness to survive. During the frequent gales, 'living smoke' – spray – would reach to the top of each mast, sheathing it in ice. In the worst of conditions, ice would cover the ship to the point where not a splinter of wood could be seen.

The Lighthouse Board was in the habit of sending out the *Verbena* on fine winter days to check that all was well with the lightship. The *Verbena* would not close the *South Shoal*, just come into view, take a look then disappear once more to home, comfort and the heady mix of companionship denied to the ten crewmen on the ship they'd squinted at then left behind. No one doubts the necessity of checking on the lightship but what casual cruelty characterised the manner in which it was done! Surely there could have been at the very least an exchange of letters.

Fog occurred with chilling regularity over the shoals and the sole device to help defeat it was the enormous bell perched ten feet above the deck. It was tolled by pulling on a rope. During one season 55 days out of 70 gave thick weather and the bell was rung once every two minutes for 12 days and nights without pause.

The fog-bell. *Century Magazine*, August, 1891.

Mostly the crew were old whalemen, accustomed to long, perilous months at sea. They did not simply present a brave face to the tedium of the life they led and to the perils they were powerless to prevent. They had to be actively courageous as well. The men conducted many a rescue, the most celebrated of these occurring in the dead of winter when they saved all 27 hands from the steamer *City of Newcastle*, which piled up on a nearby shoal, slipped off and sank stern first.

During the First World War, the vessel manning the station – now named simply *Nantucket* – on several occasions also seized the chance to perform an active life-saving role rather than a preventive one. In 1916, the German submarine U-53 regularly patrolled close to the lightship and sank many merchant vessels. The crew of the *Nantucket* rescued hundreds of men and at one stage had 115 seamen from torpedoed ships crammed on board.

It was a station notorious for the number of near collisions. One skipper of an early lightship complained: 'Some of the steamers passed very close aboard during fog, a few times almost grazing us.'

Commissioned in May 1931, *LS 117* was assigned to Nantucket. The pride of the lighthouse establishment's fleet of 36 light vessels, she was 135 feet long, of very heavy construction and carried the latest aids to navigation including radio beacon and submarine oscillator. Her electric light was of the incandescent type. Motive power was provided by oil-burning steam engines.

In 1933, she had her first brush with disaster, being dealt a glancing blow by the liner USS *Washington*. It was the overture to a terrible main event. The night of May 14th, 1934 was an anxious one for the crew. As *LS 117* rode to anchor the sea was glassy calm but fog enveloped their world. Several times in the course of the night, vessels swept by dangerously close and the lightship skipper, Captain George W. Braithwaite, ordered every man to remain awake and to don his lifejacket. The ship's lifeboat was kept ready for instant use.

Come morning, *LS 117's* steam-driven fog signal was still screaming out its warning whistle, the light still winked a glaring eye. Also, as was the practice in such conditions, the little ship's radio beacon was in operation.

The radio beacon was a new wonder of the world. Since men first went down to the sea in ships they had dreamed of an eye with the magic power to see through the thickest fog, to remain constant and unblinking through the fiercest of storms. Now they had one. The beacon was an identifying signal using a set of Morse code letters – in this case four dashes – to indicate the presence of a specific lightship and to offer mariners the means of achieving a navigational 'fix'. This could be done by taking bearings electronically on one or more stations sending out such signals.

Several bearings, from other ships or from lighthouses, would result in a 'fix' while just one bearing would at least give the direction of the signal source and identify that source. The signals worked to a schedule in clear weather but were in continuous operation where visibility was less than five miles.

The submarine oscillator, suspended below the keel, sent out a series of electrical pulses which pushed sound waves through the water in such a way as to enable navigators aboard oncoming ships to check their distance to the lightship by means

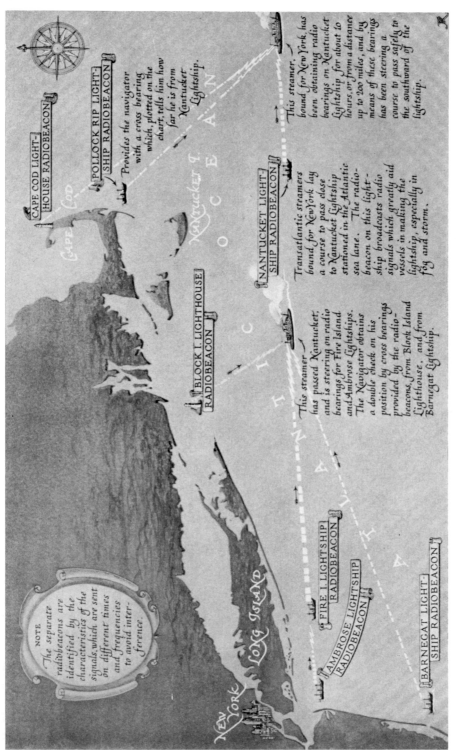

The sketch demonstrates how radio beacons assist navigators bound for New York. In this example, the Cape Cod lighthouse beacon is used in association with light vessel beacons. *The National Geographic Magazine*, August, 1936.

One example of the subsea vibrator. Redrawn from *Revue Technique du Service des Phares et Balises et de la Navigation* No. 82, June, 1989.

of a stopwatch calibrated in miles. For practical purposes the radio beacon signal, travelling at 186,000 miles per second, was calculated to be received in the same instant it was sent out. As soon as this was heard the stopwatch was started. When the subsea signal, travelling at 4,800 feet per second was received via a phonic 'ear' in the hull, the watch at that moment showed the distance to the lightship. The range of these underwater pulses could occasionally exceed 50 miles.

With all of their equipment working well, the 11-man crew of the *Nantucket* should not have been subjected to the near misses of the previous night. But they were never alone for long in the fog. Now carving through the Atlantic at 16 knots, the sister ship of the *Titanic*, the 47,000-ton Royal Mail Steamer *Olympic*, was bearing down upon them, steering to the radio beacon.

Officially frowned upon but widely used, this practice was undoubtedly one of the reasons for the number of close shaves endured by successive *Nantucket* ships. Vessels would veer off at the last moment, leaving the lightship dancing angrily in their wash. No such change of course took place aboard the *Olympic*.

Suddenly the great liner materialised out of the grey gloom. For those men on the *Nantucket* who witnessed the onrushing prow of the ship it must have seemed like a mighty axe swinging down upon them. There would barely have been time to gasp. At 10.06, the British giant struck *LS 117* amidships, slicing her in half. The two sections of the lightship slid off into the murk, desperately injured men clinging to the wreckage. There had been no chance to use the lifeboat. During a three-hour search, boats lowered from the *Olympic* picked up seven of the crew. Three later died of their injuries, leaving just four survivors, including Captain Braithwaite.

Captain John W. Binks, Master of the *Olympic*, who had taken his barely -scratched ship into New York with its flag at half-mast, told the inquiry there that his course had indeed been set by the radio beacon from *LS 117* but he claimed it was done in such a way as to keep the lightship three points off his starboard bow. The officers on duty told how they first heard the lightship's fog whistle eight minutes before impact. All on the bridge had agreed it appeared to sound several points off to starboard. Minutes later, their bow lookout roared a warning that the lightship was dead ahead. The *Olympic's* engines were thrown into reverse but it was far too late. Although the collision had yet to occur, the random arithmetic combining the awesome physics of speed and distance had already subtracted *LS 117* from the list of living ships.

Chief Wireless Officer on the liner, Frank Clark, told the inquiry that for nearly a whole year he had been unable to achieve a 'fix' using radio beacons from the *Pollock Rip* lightship and another of the Cape Cod lightships (probably the ship marking either the Stonehorse or Handkerchief shoals) as well as the *Nantucket*. The only signal he received was from *LS 117*. He claimed that alterations in signal codes had rendered reception of either of these signals impossible.

But there was no doubt where blame for the collision lay, particularly since the Second District of the US Lighthouse Authority, from their headquarters at Chelsea, Massachusetts, had just 13 days before issued a Notice to Mariners warning ships to steer well clear of the lightship. The inquiry concluded: 'Collision due solely to fault and negligence of the *Olympic* and those in charge of her.'

The RMS *Olympic* in the act of running down the *Nantucket* lightship (*LS 117*) during a morning of heavy fog in May, 1934. Photograph from the original painting by Charles Mazoujian reproduced courtesy of the US Coastguard Public Affairs Staff, Washington DC.

Owners of the liner, the Oceanic Steam Navigation Company (parent company of the White Star Line), settled the case before it came to court. They paid $500,000 to have a replacement lightship built and to compensate families of the lost crewmen.

The echoes of this event, faint as they now are, stubbornly refuse to die away. In their book *The Riddle of the Titanic*, published in 1996 by Orion Books Ltd., co-authors Robin Gardiner and Dan Van Der Vat present a theory linking the *Olympic* with the *Titanic* in an astonishing manner. Before the *Titanic* steamed out into the Atlantic from Southampton on her first and last voyage, she and the *Olympic* were both docked in Belfast.

The theory that the liners' nameplates were interchanged is discussed at length, not least because it would have been greatly to the advantage of the White Star Line at that time to make the switch. Thus with the covert connivance of a few screw nails, the careers of the sumptuously appointed sisters may have been reversed. If true, this argument precipitates the *Olympic* against an iceberg in the world's most notorious shipping disaster on 14th and 15th April, 1912, with the loss of most of her passengers and crew. The ship that made matchwood of *LS 117* then, was the *Titanic* herself!

The new 149-foot *Nantucket* – *LS 112* – was launched in 1936 at the Pusey and Jones Shipyard at Wilmington, Delaware to replace the spare lightship *LS 106*, which had been rushed into place within 24 hours of the destruction of her predecessor. *LS 112* was the first of what were considered the unsinkable lightships.

She was a floating fortress, at 915 tons displacement weight the biggest lightship ever built in the USA and at that time the biggest anywhere. The hull was fashioned from armour plate, enclosing 43 watertight compartments. The bow and stern were double-plated. Her light, at 68 feet above the loaded waterline, was the highest of any lightship then afloat. Although just one light was in use at any one time the system was 'double-proofed' with a light on both mastheads, each capable of giving the required three flashes of one second each, followed by a two-second eclipse.

In addition to the full range of radio gear, a short-range pulse was able to transmit a musical note warning vessels that they were within 15 miles of the lightship. This was an instruction to 'watch it!' From any point below deck, a complex of ladders and access doors allowed crewmen safe passage topside.

For even such a monarch among lightships, the Atlantic in winter proved a formidable foe. On the morning of January 23rd, 1936 she was ripped from her moorings and spent a desperate 28 hours battling a hurricane. The absence of the lightship from her station presented the lighthouse authorities with a major problem. Shipping was warned that *LS 112* was out of position but this was nowhere near good enough. The Nantucket shoals had to be marked without delay. A tender vessel was dispatched from Woods Hole, Cape Cod, to act as a temporary replacement but she could make no headway in the conditions and had to return to port.

The Coastguard patrol boat *Mojave* set out on the same mission and managed to get 'on station' where she remained until the lightship was located and towed back into place. As soon as a proper relief lightship could be substituted, the storm-damaged *LS 112* was taken into Boston for repair. *LS 112* was retired in 1975. She is currently owned by the Intrepid Sea-Air-Space Museum in New York City. At her berth on the waterfront she is open to the public and still occasionally ventures out into Long Island Sound.

A number of lightships dotted the Cape Cod coastline. *Cross Rip* was one, anchored close inshore in Nantucket Sound. The ships serving there had more than their fair share of drama and tragedy. On the night of December 27th, 1867,

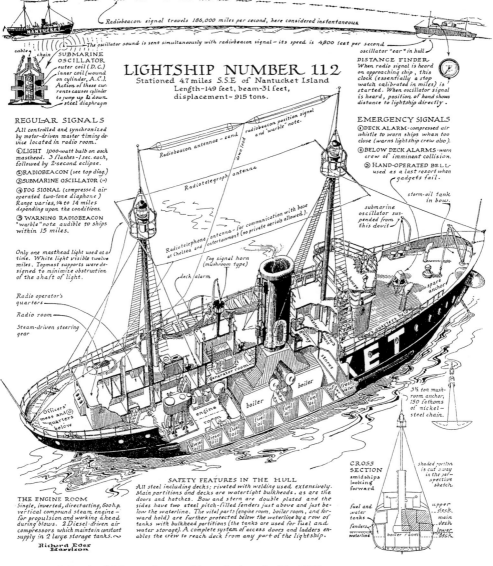

Annotated sketch of *LS 112*, the new *Nantucket* launched in 1936.

The lightship *Nantucket*, at her former berth as a floating museum in Portland, Maine, USA. She is now berthed on the New York City waterfront.
Photograph Kevin Shields.

the *Cross Rip* parted her mooring during a south-westerly gale. On the verge of foundering with five feet of water in the hold and rising, and with her upperworks encased in ice, the ship provided just enough of a platform to enable a cargo vessel to rescue the crew. Minutes later the lightship slipped under the waves.

There was no means of contacting the shore as the rescue vessel shambled slowly south towards her destination – New Orleans. With all hope gone among relatives and colleagues of the *Cross Rip* crew, a telegraph message from Louisiana more than a month later revealed the docking of the trader in New Orleans and the safe arrival of all hands.

LS 6 was not so lucky. On February 5th, 1918, observers on shore reported seeing the old wood-built vessel swept off her mooring by a field of wind-blown ice. The ship had neither engine nor sails and was not equipped with radio. Precisely what happened to *LS 6* and her six-man crew remains a riddle although 15 years after she disappeared, pieces of oak planking and part of a windlass believed to be from the lost lightship were sucked up by a dredger in Vineyard Sound.

LIGHT BITES

Whales were sometimes visitors to the lightships. They came to know the ships since they were always in the same place. Navigation marks maybe, on long migrations. The *North Carr* had such callers who used the ship as a scratching post. The giant mammals would scrape their backs along the hull, a tactile aquatherapy which may have helped to dislodge marine parasites. Crew members grew to dread a whale 'blowing' alongside. They all had bad breath – the whales that is!

———————————

The *Abertay*, also in Scottish waters, was a frequent haven for exhausted birds. This was not an unusual role for lightships but on one occasion in winter a flight of land birds found refuge on the ship in the Tay estuary. The galley stove of the *Abertay* was against an outside bulkhead and the birds collected so tightly on the other side of the steel plating that they formed a ball. The Master, John Gillies, was able to pick them up, still in a ball, and carry them inside. The birds were given the freedom of the ship. They perched on books being read by the crew, were fed and watered in the galley and snuggled down for the night to be released, fresh and rested in the morning.

———————————

On a light vessel it was essential to get along with your shipmates. Confined in the same tiny area sometimes for months on end if bad weather held up reliefs, nerve ends could begin to fray, the irritating habits of others assuming gigantic proportions. It is astonishing that so little friction actually occurred. But on one Nantucket lightship the Master and the Chief Engineer grew to loathe one another to such an extent that if they were ever required by their hours of duty to take their meals at the same time, a curtain was drawn across the centre of the dining table to keep them apart.

———————————

South Africa's *Roman Rock* light vessel in False Bay, near the Simonstown naval base was a desperate assignment. The only lightship ever used in South African waters, the *Roman Rock* was on station between 1845 and 1861. Two men worked the ship, which was little more than a hulk, with two more as relief crew ashore. They were expected to keep a watch between them 24 hours a day and carry out the endless daily tasks of maintaining a working ship, especially one which was barely seaworthy. Not surprisingly, the men were often found drunk on duty, were dismissed for the offence and since no-one else would do the work, were just as frequently rehired.

LV XX (Vyl)

*O*n December 3rd, 1909, a storm blew up from the south-west, unleashing its full fury upon the string of lightships anchored off the Danish port of Esbjerg. These included *LV XX* (Danish lightships of the day bore Roman numerals), newly-built of matured oak at Rasmus Moller's yard in Faaborg. She was stationed about five nautical miles south-west of the *Vyl* shallows.

By noon, the wind had risen to hurricane force with waves breaking over the ship. At 3.45 pm a huge sea smashed the capstan housing to pieces and at the same time the mooring parted about 12 fathoms (23 metres) outside the hawse-hole. The ship broached to and the crew raised sail immediately, setting the outer fore-staysail and the spanker (a fore-and-aft sail set on the aftermost mast). At the same time the Master, 49-year-old Julius Sofus Jensen, telegraphed to Blaavands Huk Lighthouse informing them that his ship was adrift and inquired whether help could be sent.

The radio facility was introduced in 1901/1902 at the lighthouse and on the North Sea lightships at the *Vyl* shallows and the Horns Rev. This development came about after a shipwreck on the Horns Rev when the entire crew of a German steamer perished. The tragedy was witnessed by the crew of the *Horns Rev* Lightship, who could not even summon help.

Captain Jensen had a fight on his hands to save his ship. In his report to the Director of the Danish Lights and Buoys Service, he wrote:

Violent waves were breaking over her all the time and made it impossible for anyone to work on deck without great danger of being washed overboard.

We could see that we were bound to run aground. At about 11 pm we were again in contact with Blaavands Huk to tell them we were still drifting northwards. We could see nothing at all because of the continuing heavy gusts of rain and hail.

At 11.45, the ship crashed into an outer bar and the starboard fresh water tank broke loose and smashed into the tank on the port side.

The ship continued to take ground and at 1 am grounded herself on Bjerregaard Beach just north of Nymindegab, Jutland.

At 2.30 am a man appeared on the beach and shouted to us that a rescue party would soon be there. They arrived at 4 am with a breeches buoy to get us off one by one.

We were then taken to the house of the receiver of wrecks, there to have dry clothes and a rest. When we left the ship she lay about a cable's length off the beach.

Apart from the Master, the crew consisted of cook Hans Jessen and Able Seamen Niels Sonnichsen, Hans Jensen, Soren Holst, Christian Thodsen and Soren B. Fischer, who had already survived a shipwreck, that of the schooner *Sophie* in 1880. His experiences didn't seem to do him any harm as he lived until the age of 91.

Seaman Thodsen had disappeared. He had not been seen by the rest of the crew since midnight and it was presumed he had been washed overboard. It was later discovered he had been crushed to death between the water tanks. *LV XX* had taken her punishment well. After being repaired in 1910 she served until the 1980s, mostly in the quieter waters of the Kattegat and never again at a North Sea station.

Dutch Lightship no. 11 was built in 1953 by the naval shipyard 'Rijkswerf' Willemsoord, Den Helder. She was blown off her anchor at the Texel by a force 10 gale in October, 1991 and ran ashore on a dyke, the 'Hondsbossche Zeewering', some 20 miles north-east of Ijmuiden. The damage sustained was severe and she was demolished where she lay a month later although the light itself was saved for a museum. The Texel station was subsequently demanned in 1977. Photograph courtesy of Jan Jaap Kruk.

The *Vyl* lightship leans on her port side on Bjerregaard Beach, December, 1909.
Photograph courtesy of Fiskeri-og Søfartsmuseet, Esbjerg.

But the North Sea had not done with *LV XX*. Having been converted into a
floating restaurant in Aarhus, Denmark, she was under tow in the summer of 1996
from Korsor to the Essex port of Tilbury when she sank in Dutch waters at the
entrance to the Stortemelk channel between the Friesian islands of Terschelling and
Vlieland on July 1st. Her four crew members escaped onto the towing vessel. Lying
on the bottom in only 12 metres of water, the former lightship, having spent so
much of her life preventing vessels from running into marine hazards, was now
herself considered a hazard to navigation. The Dutch salvage company Smit Lloyd,
using their Number 6 lifting barge, raised her on July 21–22 and floated her into
Rotterdam.

The *Graadyb* Lightship, motorised lightship no 2, off Esbjerg, Denmark. Built in 1916, she was subsequently sold to Dragør Yacht Club in 1978. Photograph of the original 1936 painting by Christian Benjamin Olsen courtesy of Fiskeri-og Søfartsmuseet, Esbjerg.

Lightships had always had a difficult time marking the Vyl Shallows. One had previously broken adrift in 1894. The station was established over a steeply sloping seabed, which placed enormous strain on the chains linking the ship with the anchor. Thicker cables were employed to counter this but it was clearly not enough. When in 1911, the *Vyl* Lightship broke loose again, the Danish authorities began to consider installing engines in their lightships so that in heavy weather, the ships could use motor power to ease the strain on the riding cable. They also reasoned that even if the ship did break loose, the vessel would be able to manoeuvre and either regain its station or perhaps reach port. These deliberations produced the nation's first motorised lightship in 1913/14. Her first Master was Julius Sophus Jensen.

Denmark built four powered lightships and, as a general rule, the Lights and Buoys Service used them on their exposed North Sea stations. The drive shafts on these ships were braked while not in use thus preventing constant movement of the propeller and therefore wear and tear.

You can try to describe life aboard ship at difficult locations but the words that really count will always be spoken or written by the people who have actually experienced it. One of these was Borge Mikkelsen who, in a letter from the *Horns Rev* Lightship in 1976 wrote:

I arrived for duty on November 24th but on account of the weather we could not carry out the exchange of crews until the afternoon of the 25th. Lightship no. 18 was on station and because of the very strong current the ship was tossing violently about, depending on the height of the waves and the strength of the wind.

Up forward, cotton waste, clothes and towels had been hung up below deck to soak up water after the night's storm.

When I had been on board a few days, the wind began to freshen towards evening and when I went off watch at 0400 next morning a force 10 gale was blowing.

Before going to bed I wrung out the cloths and towels that had been hung up under the deck in the fo'c'sle where I slept.

After I had been lying for a few hours trying to sleep I was freezing cold and my teeth were chattering.

I then discovered to my astonishment that my mattress, bedclothes and underclothes were soaking wet – water was running off the deck and pouring down the bulkheads. A check of the fo'c'sles revealed that only four bunks were tolerably dry and only two completely usable.

In the course of my first week on board the wind again got up to about force 10. At about 0400 the ship rolled so violently that I was thrown out of my bunk and landed on the table, ending halfway up the opposite bulkhead. For a moment I thought the ship had capsized. I could hear water pouring in over the deck through the closed hatch to the companionway and down the ladder. What it was like to be outside in weather like this, going on watch or to the toilets can easily be imagined. The toilets were in the doghouses aft.

On November 18th, Motorised Lightship No. 1 came on station which was a considerable improvement, as the events of January 3rd proved.

After we had come on board on January 2nd, the wind began to freshen towards evening and when I went off watch at 2400 it was force 8. The ship was rolling heavily and I could not relax or fall asleep. Unfortunately I belong to that group of people who can only sleep lying on their side and this was impossible. I had to lie on my stomach with legs spreadeagled, or on my back in the same position. I think transverse bunks would have been better on this station.

The lightship had been rolling constantly, with the covering boards often under water and it was impossible to get a proper sleep. You lie tensed up in your bunk, hanging on fast and are more tired when you are roused than when you went to bed. You feel it most in the back and legs.

When the watch was called on January 3rd, the wind was blowing force 11. We had to put our oilskins on straight away and go on deck. We managed to get all the metal hatches on the doors to the deckhouse bolted to. We put extra lashings on the motor boat and the lifeboat.

The wind continued to rise and by about 1000 it was force 12–127.8 kilometres an hour.

The waves were breaking over the lightship, some more violent than others. The strange thing about these waves was that they often came from three directions at once. One wave hit the deckhouse with such force that one could almost see it shift a few millimetres. The TV aerial broke off and fell down and a section of the breakwater on the starboard side was smashed off.

One wave hit the motor boat so violently that the hook on the end of the wire attached to the gripe* was straightened out – and the hook was very heavy and solid. At the same time part of the gunwhale was knocked out of position.

With a concerted effort we got the motor boat lashed fast again but just at that moment we saw one of these huge waves rearing up off the starboard bow.

We just managed to spring for cover behind the deckhouse and hang onto the stays before the wave broke over us. Oilskins are not much use in that kind of situation.

We have just heard that the lightship station is probably to be moved about five nautical miles further out in the North Sea and we hope this will mean the ship will be in a more stable position.

Today, Motorised Lightship No. 1 is a museum ship at Esbjerg, one of several light vessels preserved in Denmark.

---

*The gripe was a heavy rope passed round the entire ship at deck height. The mooring chain was attached to it so that the whole vessel was held fast by the chain. Being flexible to a degree, the gripe acted as an efficient shock absorber in heavy weather. This method was eventually replaced by elastic compressors fitted onto the foredeck.

LIGHT BITES

An intriguing explanation of how reflectors first came to be used in lighthouse and lightship lanterns appeared in the long-defunct publication *Glasgow Mechanic's Magazine*. Quoted in *The Times* of November 10th, 1824, the magazine ran a piece entitled: 'Lighthouses in England, Use of Mirrors'. It read:

'The use of mirrors for reflecting lighthouses in England is of very recent date and owes its origin to a trivial circumstance which was as follows: At a meeting of mathematicians at Liverpool, one of the members proposed to lay a wager that he could read a paragraph of a newspaper at 10 yards' distance by the light of a farthing candle. The wager was laid and the proposer covered the inside of a wooden dish with pieces of a looking glass fastened in with glazier's putty, placed this reflector behind his candle and won the wager. One of the company viewed this experiment with a philosophic eye. This was Captain Hutchison, the local Dockmaster. With him originated these reflecting lighthouses in Liverpool which were built in 1763. In his treatise on Practical Seamanship he wrote: 'We have made, and have in use here at Liverpool, reflectors of 1, 2 and 3 feet focus and 3, 5½, 7½ and 12 feet diameter, the three small ones made of tin soldered together and the largest of wood covered with a looking glass; the two large ones, called the Sea Lights, leading through the channel from the sea till the two Hoydale lights are brought in a line that leads to a very good roadstead to lie till it is a proper time to proceed to Liverpool.'

Although the *Nore* Lightship, moored in the Thames in 1732, is generally recognized as the world's first lightship, reports from ancient times credit the Romans with introducing the principle. Just before the birth of Christ, Roman galleys were said to be engaged in anti-pirate patrols in the eastern Mediterranean, showing fires from time to time in baskets atop their masts to indicate to mariners that the port they were heading for was safe to approach (i.e. it had not been occupied by corsairs). But the galleys were built of wood, the sails made of highly flammable cloth, the rigging of rope. The notion that fires were lit on top of gyrating wooden masts, spewing out sparks and embers onto a ship baked tinder-dry by the Mediterranean sun has to be many a sea mile wide of the mark.

LS 83
(Blunt's Reef)

*A*lthough built as one of a series of five similar ships at Camden, New Jersey, on the eastern side of the United States, this vessel spent her entire career on the west coast, serving at all five Pacific light vessel stations, sometimes as a relief lightship.

Under the command of Captain E.M. Trott, the new $90,000 lightship, driven by a powerful steam engine and carrying 150 tons of coal, voyaged south in the company of another lightship, LS 76, from the U.S. Lighthouse Establishment at Tomkinsville, Staten Island through the Strait of Magellan at the wild southern tip of the American continent then northwards again to San Francisco, arriving on June 4th, 1905. The trip had taken 110 days, covering a distance exceeding half the circumference of the globe.

With the official opening of the Panama Canal in June, 1920, at least part of the process was conducted in reverse, with lightships built on the Pacific coast sometimes going through the canal to take up stations in Atlantic waters.

LS 83's first assignment was Blunt's Reef. This dangerous area lies three miles off Cape Mendocino, just over 100 miles north of San Francisco. The hazard is a series of hidden ledges and rocks about half a mile offshore. The irregular bottom and strong currents make for turbulent water over the reef in almost any weather. The lightship's anchorage was approximately two miles to the seaward side of the rocks, in 30 fathoms of water. *LS 83* was blown off station no fewer than six times in 1905 and 1906. In 1915, she was driven two miles by winds gusting to 110 mph.

But a moment of glory not given to many lightships was close at hand. On June 14th, 1916, the San Francisco-Portland Steamship Company vessel *Bear* was groping her way down the coast through dense fog on her regular run from Portland, Oregon to San Francisco. It was a typical summer 'pea souper' with the waters of the Pacific, chilled by the California current sweeping down from sub-Arctic latitudes, cooling the warm air and producing an upward precipitation of moisture – fog.

The sea was calm and the *Bear's* 127 passengers were all snuggled down for the night. It was an anxious time for those of the 84-strong crew on duty. Five men were on watch, including the Master, Captain L.M. Nopander, one of the most respected and competent navigators on the Pacific coast. The *Bear's* fathometer equipment for checking the depth of the water was in constant operation. As a double check, Nopander had a leadsman employed at the bow, calling out the depth showing on his line. When the water shoaled to 28-30 fathoms, the ship was headed further offshore until there was no bottom sounding. Another course alteration turned the *Bear* slightly to the south, resuming her base course.

LS 83 during her spell as the San Francisco lightship.

Here, nature had played a cruel trick on the *Bear*. The earthquake of 1906 is best remembered for causing the destruction by fire of San Francisco. But it also wrenched and tore the seabed in the area of Cape Mendocino, creating numerous sink holes. It seems certain that the 'no bottom' sounding was taken over one of these pits. Far from being in deep water, his ship was in deadly danger.

A few minutes after his last change of course, the *Bear* piled up on Sugar Loaf Point, the outermost pinnacle of Blunt's Reef. The tremendous impact as the steamer wedged herself onto the rocks occurred at 10.15 pm and jolted both passengers and off-duty crewmen out of their sleep. Terrified passengers scrambled onto the deck, still in their nightclothes. The initial panic was quickly controlled by the crew as Captain Nopander checked the integrity of his ship's hull. He found the outer skin pierced, with water flooding the forward compartments. The watertight bulkhead for'ard of the engine room was doing its job however and the dynamos housed there were undamaged, allowing radio signals to be sent. The inner part of the *Bear's* double bottom was still watertight. Nopander tried several times to back her off the rocks. The *Bear* would not budge. Now the skipper sent off an SOS call and began to prepare his passengers to abandon ship.

Captain Nopander and three of his crew decided to stay on board. These included Chief Engineer John F. Jackson, who had been on board the liner *Columbia* which was sunk in a collision with the loss of 73 lives off Cape Mendocino on July 21st, 1907. Jackson's experience paled into insignificance compared with that of the purser, C.F. Heywood, who was now enduring his fourth wreck. Included in his personal dossier of disaster was the wreck of the steamer *George W. Elder* near Goble on the lower Columbia River on January 21st, 1905 and just five weeks later, the fire which destroyed the steamer *Oregon* off Crescent City on the north California coast.

Now another *Oregon* – the battleship of that name – along with the steamer *Grace Dollar* and the Lumbermen's Association tug *Relief* from Eureka, was already responding to the emergency call and trying to grope her way to the scene. From the bridge of the battleship the officers could not even see their own flagstaff. Other vessels joined the search, the steamer *Queen* and the Coastguard lifeboat *Liberator*.

On board the *Bear* the ship's 14 lifeboats were cleared away on the lee side at 11.40 pm amid much cheerful singing. Later, as he looked back on the worst crisis of his career, Captain Nopander observed: 'The crew and passengers were the coolest I ever saw.' The flotilla of boats was sent off into the grey night with orders to make for the lightship four miles away, from which they stood the best chance of being picked up by the rescue ships now en route.

In the dark, three lifeboats became separated from the group. They headed for shore. Hearing the waves pounding on the beach but unable to see, the survivors in their tiny lifeboats entered the boiling surf. One, carrying 34 people including many children, overturned. What then occurred was little short of a miracle. In the tumbling, freezing water and pitch blackness every single child made it safely to the shore.

One youngster owed his life to vaudeville entertainer Agnes Loftus, who pulled him and his mother, Mrs George H. Learned, from underneath the lifeboat as it lay stranded on the beach. Just two crewmen and three passengers drowned. Miss Loftus herself had almost died.

She recalled:

I was in Number Five lifeboat. We had not pulled very far from the Bear when a big comber caught us squarely on the beam. In a twinkling we capsized. It seemed to me I went down 1000 feet. When I came to the surface gasping for breath a woman grabbed me in a bear hug around my neck. I fought her off and we both went under. I got to the surfce again but I don't know what happened to the other woman.

Just as I felt I could no longer keep afloat one of the oarsmen grabbed me by the hair and kept my head above water. I must have fainted and when I came to I was on the shore.

The survivors from all three lifeboats were now on the beach, soaked and chilled. Some built windbreaks from driftwood, others dug holes in the sand and crawled inside. First Assistant Engineer John Hansen dispatched a crew member to the nearest community, Capetown, but it was daybreak before he returned with some of the residents, mostly farmers, who brought blankets, clothing and food with them.

On board *LS 83*, which would not be equipped with radio until 1918, the lookout was probably wondering why he was on deck at all. Even with the ship's two white kerosene-burning lights glaring above his head, he could see nothing on this damp, miserable night. The steam chime fog whistle, mounted on a pedestal between the funnel and the afterdeck house, was screaming out its distinctive message – an operation which used vast amounts of the precious coal and fresh water supplies on board.

Suspended on a line 25 feet below the surface, the underwater fog signal was in operation. The introduction of this ingenious device, first used in the United States, stemmed from experiments conducted in 1841 on Lake Geneva, Switzerland, a country with no coastline. Using a bell, the tests were undertaken to establish the suitability of water as a medium for transmitting sound. They revealed an exceptional capability, far exceeding in range and speed sound signals through the air. There was also greater dependability, air-borne sound being subject to wide variations according to wind-speed and temperature. Little practical use was made of this data until the 19th century had almost gone.

LS 83's underwater equipment consisted of a bell with a mechanically operated tongue which in monotonous succession struck eight times, followed by three seconds of silence, then struck three times more, thus giving the number of the lightship. The code, sprinting through the sea at 4½ times the speed of sound through the air, could be detected more than 10 miles away by ships equipped with microphones situated below the waterline and transmitted to earpieces resembling old-style telephones. When not in operation the submarine bell was stored on deck in a cradle and encased in a canvas-covered box pierced by ventilation holes.

On this bone-chilling night however, the whistle was the lifesaver. The passengers and crew in the lifeboats had been groping around for hours trying to find the lightship. Only when they picked up the sound of the whistle were they sure of their direction. It was now 1.30 am. The first things heard by the lightship lookout were human cries, then the sweep of oars. A lifeboat swam into view and drew alongside. The man on deck rang the emergency bell and Captain Henry Pierotti and the crew of *LS 83* swung into action. A ladder was lowered and men, women and children began to clamber up to safety. Another lifeboat arrived, then another.

In seas which were beginning to chop in the rising wind, one passenger, Mrs Irene K. Leahy, fell out of a lifeboat and was picked up again only with the greatest difficulty. Mrs Leahy had vanished into the fog and it was some time before she was located again. Had she not been an accomplished swimmer the number of casualties must have risen by one.

Soon more than 100 shivering survivors from the wreck of the *Bear* were crowded onto a 135-foot ship designed to hold just 11 crew members. Blankets and hot coffee were hurriedly produced. By this time, nine lifeboats from the *Bear* were tied up to the lightship. At 3 am the *Liberator* arrived just as the tug *Relief* came alongside with survivors from the last two lifeboats.

Constant wireless contact between the *Grace Dollar* and the *Oregon* had brought the smaller vessel to the scene. The captain of the battleship, with its 26-foot draught, had prudently decided his ship could not take an active part in proceedings in an area studded with treacherous shallows. By 7.40 am the lightship's grateful guests had all been transferred to the *Grace Dollar*. By 8.45 am normal lightship duties had resumed. But the crew carried with them a glow of awareness that but for the presence that night of *LS 83*, the final death toll of five would surely have been many times that number.

A sad footnote to the *Bear* mishap concerns two further casualties. A prize $7000 stallion drowned, as did a fearless crew member – the ship's dog – which had vainly tried to reach the shore with a line from the *Bear*.

LS 83 continued to have an eventful career, being rammed by the steamer *Del Norte* in 1920 and having to be towed to San Francisco for major repair work. A later *Blunt's Reef* lightship took aboard the crew of another ship, the tanker *Emidio*. They made their way to the lightship in lifeboats after the tanker had been torpedoed by a Japanese submarine off Cape Mendocino on December 20th, 1941. This incident led to the blacking out of coastal aids to navigation and the withdrawal from service of most of America's lightships.

During the Second World War, *LS 83* became a patrol gunboat, her crew rising to 40. The main armament was a three-inch gun on the foredeck. She also carried two 50-calibre machine guns and an afterdeck 'Y' gun for firing depth charges. Before she was decommissioned on July 18th, 1960, *LS 83* put in a spell marking the Swiftsure Bank off Seattle, Washington, during which time she was painted yellow with black lettering to avoid any possible confusion with the *Umatilla* Lightship 22 miles further south.

The oldest surviving lightship in America, *LS 83* had been gradually deteriorating in Seattle, where she is the responsibilty of the Northwest Seaport Museum. The museum staff have not been idle however and are striving to restore her. Their efforts have been endorsed by the Royal Victoria and Seattle Yacht clubs and by the Mayor of Victoria, Canada. Joint Canadian/American plans include placing *LS 83* once a year on the old Swiftsure station during the Swiftsure Classic yacht race, so raising the prospect of a manned lightship at sea again, however briefly.

LIGHT BITES

The crew of *LS 53*, the *Charleston* Lightship off the coast of South Carolina, kept a cat called Tom. Described as 'a hefty old tomcat' he had been born on the ship. His assignment – eradication of rodents and amusement of the crew. The Master of the ship thought of him as a typical sailor. 'When the boat comes to dock he'll go ashore, get into a few scraps and come aboard next morning with scratches and general evidence of having made a night of it. But you may be sure he'll never let the ship go without him.' *The Lighthouse Digest* of the Shore Village Museum, Rockland, Maine, June, 1994.

The foghorn on many lightships delivered a double note, one high, one low, with a full octave separating the notes. The reason may be found in an address to the Society of Arts in London on March 5th, 1902 by Mr E. Price Edwards on the subject of sound signals at sea. He compared the merits of the new low note seven-inch disc siren with the higher-pitched cylinder sirens during experiments carried out at the Trinity House fog signal station at St Catherine's Point, Isle of Wight. It was found that on one occasion in fine weather with a light easterly breeze the low note could be heard 20 miles away. Higher-pitched signals were lost at half that distance. On another day with a force 4 wind and rough sea, the low note was at a disadvantage and reached just 1.25 miles. Curious silent areas were mentioned, the sounds beginning to die away from either siren or horn until they became fainter and even inaudible, recovering in strength when the three-mile line had been passed.

Crew members aboard the lightships of most countries took turns at cooking. However, in the latter days of the American lightship service, the vessels carried professional cooks who were trained at the US Coastguard School for Cooks and Bakers.

LV Comet
(Daunt Rock)

*A*s darkness fell on the 10th of February, 1936, the crew of the *Comet*, marking the Daunt Rock just off Cork (Queenstown) Harbour on the south coast of Ireland, were preparing themselves for another night of heavy weather. They had been on the receiving end of a south-easterly gale for three days and it showed no signs of abating.

At about 1 am on the 11th, the mate of the lightship, J. Scanlon, was on watch with fellow crewmen Arnopp, Busher and Swift. The *Comet* was shipping heavy seas when the portable fire pump broke loose from its lashings on deck and disappeared overboard. Then the deck flange of the cabin funnel became badly strained and the deck damaged in this area.

Almost immediately afterwards the ship fell off into the trough of a wave and the men on watch realised she had parted her moorings. All hands were called and began the difficult and dangerous task of clearing away the spare anchor. It was essential this anchor be dropped in a hurry or the helpless ship must surely pile up on the very rock she was assigned to guard. It took just ten minutes for the anchor to hit the sea floor – an extraordinary feat of seamanship in the conditions. The *Comet* checked and was held, only just in time. Now the lightship's main light had to be extinguished. The 'off station' lights – one red at the stem, one red at the stern – were lit. Flares were exhibited. One crewman burned his hand badly during this exercise but continued to carry out his duties.

The *Comet's* first distress signal was picked up by the German tug *Seafalke* from where it was relayed to Burnham radio station, the Commissioners of Irish Lights and other shipping in the vicinity.

HMS Tenedos, a Royal Navy destroyer then based at Queenstown, put to sea in a blinding rainstorm to attempt to pinpoint the position of the lightship. The steamer *Inishfallen* was also passing out of the harbour on her way to Fishguard when she heard of the *Comet's* plight. Full of passengers as she was, the *Inishfallen* joined in the search, one report having reached the rescue vessels that the lightship had sunk. However, her spare anchor was still holding and she was spotted at 10 am. Massive seas were exploding over the *Comet*, whose crew had not slept more than an hour during the last 48. The ship was just a quarter of a mile from the Daunt Rock.

Further east, the lifeboat at Ballycotton had received the distress call at 8 am. The lifeboat secretary, Robert Mahoney, faced an appalling dilemma – to go or not to go. The harbour at Ballycotton was experiencing unheard-of conditions. Mahoney described the harbour waters as 'a seething cauldron'. Stones weighing a ton were being wrenched from the quay and 'tossed around like sugar lumps'. But his coxswain, Patrick Sliney, had quietly been assembling the crew. The first Mahoney knew about the lifeboat launch was when he saw the boat crashing through the maelstrom in the harbour mouth. Sliney, perhaps fearful of being ordered to stay put, had taken his own decision to respond to the emergency call. Those people who watched her go went to church to pray.

As they headed for the Daunt Rock the lifeboat was shipping such vast quantities of water into the after cockpit with almost every following sea that Sliney had to carry out a continous head count of his crew. The lifeboat fell into the trough of one wave with such force that the men felt the engines must surely smash through the bottom of the boat. In the shocking conditions they were unable to find the black-hulled *Comet* and decided to call in at Queenstown for information. It was 11 am. By noon they were standing by the lightship along with *HMS Tenedos*.

The *Inishfallen* resumed her voyage to Fishguard. *Tenedos* agreed to stay with the *Comet* all night while the lifeboat put into Queenstown again, for more ropes and food. It was now early on the 12th and they forced their way back to the lightship through towering waves. *Tenedos* now left the scene.

The *Comet* crew had elected to stay with their ship to continue marking the rock for other seafarers but they were now in real danger of being smashed into it themselves. Another day and night of the seemingly endless ordeal had yet to be endured as the freezing, ravenous crews battled against the kind of weather not one of these seasoned seamen had ever experienced.

Driven by a pressing need for fuel, the lifeboat returned to Queenstown at 9 am on the 13th. Her crew had been standing by for 25½ hours, seas constantly breaking over their craft. A hitch in the supply of petrol delayed their departure from Queenstown and it was 4 pm before she was under way. When they reached the lightship again, they found the lighthouse tender *Isolda* in attendance.* Precisely what they did not need was that which ensued. The weather deteriorated still further to the disbelief of all. At about 8 pm a huge sea buried the lightship, carrying away the forward of her off-station lights.

The lifeboat coxswain was becoming increasingly concerned for the men on the *Comet*. At 9.30 pm he took his boat round the lightship's stern and by searchlight, could see the crew, lifebelts on, huddled together on deck. Their ship had been dragging her emergency anchor and was now just 60 yards from the Daunt Rock. If the anchor chain parted there would be no time for the lifeboat crew to do anything but watch the destruction of the *Comet* and her crew. It was time for a decision. Sliney resolved to take off the men.

For a fresh lifeboat crew this would have been a monumental task. For the exhausted men on the Ballycotton lifeboat, it was hazardous almost beyond comprehension. The *Comet* was behaving like an animal caught in a trap. She plunged wildly at the end of her cable, rolling 30°–40° with her stern whipping around viciously. She was fitted with rolling chocks which projected about two feet beyond her sides and they constituted an obvious peril for the lifeboat. Sliney informed the *Comet* crew by loud hailer what he intended to do.

Getting astern of his target, the coxswain took his boat along the port side at full tilt, checked her for a second then sent his engines full astern. In the instant of relative immobility, the men on the lightship had to jump. Six times the manoeuvre was repeated and on the last of these, members of the lifeboat crew had to grab the two remaining crewmen still clinging to the rails of their ship. They had neither the time nor the inclination to ask their permission.

The two lamplighters (see p31) were slightly injured in the process but although the lifeboat *was* damaged in one bone-jarring collision with the lightship – the man working the searchlight leaping clear just in time – the *Comet* crew were all

The rescue of the crew of the *Comet*.
RNLI photograph from an original painting by Bernard Finegan Gribble.

successfully transferred. They had been driven to the outer edge of endurance by six days of unrelieved torment and one man finally cracked, became hysterical, and had to be restrained.

The very next morning however, the entire crew were taken back to the *Comet*, the weather having eased. The *Isolda* managed to tow the ship into Queenstown where new moorings were hastily produced and temporary repairs made. By 4.45 pm the following day, in the best traditions of the lightship service, the *Comet* was back on station, resuming her role as the mariner's friend, posted to seaward of the Daunt Rock. The rock would continue to be marked by manned lightships for another 38 years. On August 30th, 1974 the last of these, *LV Osprey*, was replaced by an electronic buoy.

The Royal National Lifeboat Institution awarded its gold medal – the Victoria Cross of the lifeboat service – to coxswain Sliney, the silver medal to the second coxswain and the motor mechanic and bronze medals to the other four members of the crew. The men of the *Comet* had been lucky. The *Puffin* Lightship sank in a storm at the same location on October 8th, 1896, taking her crew of seven with her.

The relatives of that crew had to endure a particularly cruel twist of the knife. They were forced to wait for days before the fate of the ship was confirmed by a diver and in the meantime a rumour to the effect that the lightship had fetched up at Tramore Bay, County Waterford with all her crew safe had received widespread credence. The Lloyds agent at Queenstown even telegraphed his main office in London to this effect.

Fate dealt the *Comet* a strange hand when she came out of service. Built in Scotland in 1904 at the Glasgow shipyard of J. Reid, she was returned to Scotland in 1965 in a deal struck with ship brokers Turner and Hickman. The 96-foot ship was converted into the pirate radio station Radio Scotland and for 20 hours a day starting at three minutes to midnight on December 31st, 1965, spent the next 19 months broadcasting on 242 metres a more or less continuous diet of pop music, scathingly referred to in those days as 'audible wallpaper'. It cost £1500 a week to run the station. This bizarre – but not unique – use for a lightship came to an end at midnight on August 14th, 1967 when the Marine Broadcasting (Offences) Bill became law, much to the disgust of the backers of Radio Scotland who claimed 60% of Scots had tuned in to their station at some point.

The Government of Harold Wilson was determined to stop what was described as 'interference' with continental broadcasting by all eight pirate radio stations operating around Britain and possibly fatal interference with emergency trans-missions. Penalties for breaching the new legislation were severe – two years' jail or a fine to be determined by the court, or both. With the exception of Radio Caroline which was able to continue for a short time off Ramsey, Isle of Man due in part to some legal oddities associated with that island, they were simultaneously sunk.

The *Comet* disc jockeys had needed good sea legs and strong stomachs to withstand the life on the four anchorages used during her spell as Radio Scotland – off Northern Ireland, in the Firth of Clyde, off Dunbar and finally near the Isle of May in the Firth of Forth, where they did two weeks aboard and one ashore.

Wreck of the Irish lightship *Puffin*, beached at Rushbrook Dock, Cork, October 1896.
Courtesy of the Commissioners of Irish Lights.

Side-on picture of the *Puffin*.
From the Maurice Wigham collection.

The *Comet* at Methil docks.
Photograph from William Flett.

According to Radio Scotland Managing Director Tommy Shields, some had been very seasick while the programmes were on the air but still managed to sound cheerful. Six of the Radio Scotland staff offered to work as unpaid volunteers to keep the show afloat but without the lifeblood of advertising, now outlawed by the Postmaster General, the station had nowhere to go but on the rocks.

When the *Comet* was towed into Methil Docks in Fife just after noon on August 18th to be stripped of radio equipment worth thousands of pounds, a crowd of 200 mostly young people watched her come in. The radio pirates did not go quietly. Their demise provoked a flood of letters to local and national newspapers, mostly attacking the 'Big Brother' attitude of the Government, who were forced to respond by setting up a pop music station, Radio One, run by the BBC. It began broadcasting on September 30th, 1967.

'Peace talks' also took place on the Isle of Man where Radio Caroline had been extremely popular, not least because local traders had done very well out of supplying the ship. Several hundred people took part in a demonstration organised by the Edinburgh Young Conservatives at The Mound, Edinburgh, in support of Radio Scotland. But the bold venture was finished and the Sunset Clan Ball for staff and supporters at the Locarno, Glasgow assumed the character of a wake.

Tommy Shields told reporters that the *Comet* had been sold to a foreign concern by the station's London office. He knew nothing of her new owners. For two weeks her skipper, Willie Fisher and an engineer, Jack Johnstone, supervised the dismantling of the radio gear. Then the *Comet* melted away from Methil towards a future no-one at the time seemed remotely interested in. For all we know, she still displaces 250 tons of exotic seawater off some far distant shore.

*The *Isolda* did not survive the Second World War. While carrying out a routine relief of the *Coningbeg* light vessel off Wexford on December 19th, 1940, she was attacked by a German bomber. The aviators could hardly fail to have seen the words Lighthouse Service in five foot high letters on her side. Six crew members died with the *Isolda*.

The Lamplighter: A report (undated) from *LV64* at the Sunk sands in the northern approaches to the River Thames provides a classic insight into the perilous life of the lamplighter.
     It reads:

It was a night when the wind screamed through the rigging, when rain and spray lashed along the deck. That was always the time that the lamps blew out. As the vessel rolled and pitched violently a man climbed aloft by the wire ladder, clinging for dear life.

He reached the swaying lantern and, after opening the door, jumped the chasm between ladder and entrance. After closing the door he held on grimly to one of the internal circular rails. The lamps swung out on their gimbals following faithfully the random, reeling motion of the floor, leaving little room to move.

He struggled to re-light the extinguished wicks as the wind howled outside, waiting to reduce his efforts to nothing. There were two to each burner. The inner one would be lit first and that would help draw the flame on the outer one. Finally, having got them all alight, he faced the supreme test: the struggle to get out of the door backwards and close it before they were blown out again. He felt a moment of panic as his foot slipped on the wet wire of the ladder. The wind clawed at him as he quickly closed the door. Rain streamed across his face.

His sole satisfaction was that he was not alone in that wild place; for along the coast other men on other light vessels were following the same demanding routine. He was grateful to reach the deck safely but he knew that after half-an-hour, maybe an hour, another gust would blow some of the lamps out again. Such was the life of a lamplighter at the Sunk in force 10.

LIGHT BITES

During a severe storm in May, 1951, *LS 79* on the Barnegat station which marked the coastal shipping lane off Barnegat Inlet in New Jersey, USA, managed to suspend the laws of physics. Once the gale had subsided it was discovered that the anchor chain had tied itself into a perfect overhand knot, right in the middle of the cable. The lighthouse tender *Sassafras* untied the knot by raising the anchor with heavy duty lifting gear. A writer in the Coastguard bulletin at the time was as lost for an explanation as anyone else. He wrote: 'The anchor at one end weighs three tons. The ship, of course, is at the other end...'

LS 79 was known to her crews as 'Ol' Barney'. The ship is moored at Camden, New Jersey where she is looked after by the Philadelphia Ship Preservation Guild.
From a watercolour by R.C. Moore in the collection of William Combs.

LV Manicouagan

*T*he gales of November, 1873 in the lower St. Lawrence River, have passed into Canadian seafaring legend. Several lightships dotted the river at that time. The 550-ton *Manicouagan* was to become heavily engaged in the dramas which unfolded in the course of that month. One of Canada's first iron lightships, she was rigged as a two-masted schooner with a square topsail on the fore. Built in England at the Stockton-on-Tees yard of Richard Duck, further data on the ship is only available courtesy of a visit by a committee from Trinity House, London in 1872 to assess the lights of the St. Lawrence.

The committee included Deputy Master of Trinity House Sir Frederick Arrow and a Captain Webb. The St. Lawrence trip constituted a tiny part of their brief which was no less than the inspection of lighthouses and fog stations throughout Canada and the United States.

As they pulled alongside the *Manicouagan* at 7 am one fine summer day, they noted the ship was painted black with her name on the stern.

They reported:

The two lights carried, one at each masthead, are small 6th order dioptric. The oil burnt is petroleum in an ordinary oil burner. The crew of the light vessel consists of a Master, Mate, engineer and six seamen, all of whom remain on board during the season (June until December) without relief.

The party was travelling aboard the single-screw steamer *Napoleon III*, a lighthouse tender and tug built on the Clyde in 1856 at the famous Robert Napier yard.

The London group wanted to test the range of the lightship's steam-driven fog whistle and made off upstream a distance of 12 miles, at which point the sound of the whistle began to die away. There was an element of irony about this test since Trinity House had always refused to equip any British lightships or lighthouses with fog whistles. This type of signal was considered too similar to the fog whistles on steamers and too wasteful of fuel.

However, the visitors studied the *Manicouagan* whistle in some detail and reported that it was activated by a boiler which burned wood at the rate of 30 lbs per hour, the whole apparatus requiring an engine room space of 25 feet by 12 feet between the bunkers. Part of the committee's deep interest may have been fuelled by the correct perception that lightships provided particularly suitable sites for fog signals, being generally beyond the echoes of the land.

As the weather deteriorated that autumn in 1873, the *Napoleon III* left Quebec under the command of Mr J.U. Gregory, Marine Agent at Quebec. It was her last trip of the season to service the lightships. Gregory had received a report that the lightships were in trouble and it soon became apparent why. A storm was raging and the river had become a nightmare to navigate, with large floes of drifting ice.

When the *Napoleon III* came across spars and wreckage where the *Upper Traverse* Lightship should have been the inevitable conclusion was reached that she had been lost with all hands. Gregory pushed on and towed another lightship, the *Lower Traverse*, to a safe anchorage. However, unknown to Gregory, the *Upper Traverse* had managed to sail to safety by herself, the wreckage spotted later identified as coming from a fully-rigged sailing vessel which had cut away part of her gear.

On November 13th, Captain Thomas Connell of the *Manicouagan* sighted a sailing ship aground near his lightship, which was itself completely surrounded by ice. Captain Connell made repeated attempts to reach the stricken vessel by manhandling a lifeboat across the ice but to no avail. He had to resort to sounding his fog whistle to try to maintain the morale of the crew on the stranded ship. On the 15th, he made another desperate effort but was able to discover only that the crew had still not been rescued.

Only with the greatest difficulty did this intrepid seaman manage to regain his own ship. It was fast becoming unsafe for the *Manicouagan* to stay on station and Captain Connell decided to weigh anchor and set sail to get his lightship as close as possible to the wreck.

He later wrote:

> *I stood down for the wreck but before I could get there the wind, coming in from the east, fell light.*
> *Being flood tide I drifted to the westward, still blowing fog alarm signals to endeavour to get an answer from the crew of the wreck. Finding all exertions unavailing, I deemed it useless to remain any longer.*

As the lightship strove to reach Quebec, a terrible passage ensued with hurricane-force winds and driving snow. The crew were often forced off the decks by sweeping seas and bitter cold. The ship became quite unmanageable at times because of ice on deck and in the rigging. Finally, the *Manicouagan* was picked up by the *Napoleon III* on November 21st.

On the 18th, the *Red Island* lightship had also weighed anchor to run for shelter but she went aground half a mile below White Island and began to suffer a pounding.

Captain Levesque of the *Red Island* recorded that:

> *...the sea was running very heavy, so thick that we could not see anything before us. I rounded the ship on to the port helm and let go the anchor; took in*

jib and foresail, all the canvas that was on her at the time and gave her chain as fast as we could; ship driving to leeward fast with gale; at 8.15 the ship was driving close to the breakers, which I now saw for the first time. I let go the second anchor, after which the ship commenced striking heavy and I saw that she was leaking in the engine room.

The crew had to lash themselves to the rigging, drenched by icy breakers. During a brief respite in the weather, the men took to the ship's one remaining boat and made sail, baling furiously to keep it afloat. They managed to reach Cacouna on the great river's southern shore. Their lightship had to be abandoned for the winter and ended up a total loss. Her replacement the following year was another lightship which had nearly sunk in a major Atlantic storm off Sambro Island, Nova Scotia and was now considered too small for that exposed location.

The *Manicouagan* incident led to a long and at times acrimonious debate about building lightships with propulsion units. His inability to aid a ship in distress had left an indelible mark on Captain Connell, who was at the forefront of the drive to have engines installed in lightships.

He wrote:

If the lightship had propelling power by steam I would have got to the wreck and could have rendered assistance to the unfortunate sufferers, if any survived, and would have reached Quebec with my ship.

Captain Connell's long-running campaign was not in vain. Canada began to build lightships with steam reciprocating machinery, the first in 1903. Some continued to be ordered from British shipyards.

LV 61
(East Dudgeon)

*I*n the early years of the Second World War, the lightships in the English Channel and off England's east coast came under constant attack from German aircraft. The first such attack was on the *Smith's Knoll* Lightship on January 11th, 1940 with subsequent raids on lightships numbering well over 100. Trinity House, who ran the lighthouse and lightship service, lost 18 lightships and unmanned light floats during the war. Some of these were simply blown out of the water, including *LV 60* (*East Oaze*), sunk with all hands in the Thames estuary.

In August 1940, at the height of the Battle of Britain, *LV 75* serving on the *South Folkestone Gate* station, was attacked by six Dornier bombers. The men were eating dinner when the bombs began to fall. The ship leapt in the water as she was hit by a bomb while machine-gun bullets tore into the fo'c'sle. The men who scrambled out onto the sloping deck were confronted by a terrible sight. The Master, his face a mask of blood, was blindly trying to clear the falls of the lifeboat. The other lifeboat had been blown to pieces. The deckhouse was a mass of crumpled plating and the only sign of two crewmen who had been on deck were part of a shoulder and an arm. Some of the rest had been wounded by shrapnel but they still managed to lower the lifeboat with the ship sinking rapidly under them. They were picked up by a speedboat.

The *North Sand Head* Lightship had an astonishing escape. Attacked by a whole flight of bombers, she sustained a large number of near misses but no hits. An examination of the ship from lantern to bilges showed she was as sound as ever.

The crew of *LV 61* on the *East Dudgeon* station underwent an ordeal which shocked the nation. They had seen many enemy aircraft and some of the German pilots had even waved to them or dipped their wings. But until the fateful morning of January 29th, 1940, they had not been under fire. That day, attacking in poor weather in the apparent belief that the British fighter cover would be grounded, the Luftwaffe raided the east coast of Britain from Shetland down to the English Channel.

At 9.30 am a Junkers 88 bomber swooped on the 52-year-old wooden ship manning the East Dudgeon station, machine-gunning and dropping nine bombs. The Master, Mr R. George and his crew of seven clambered into a lifeboat and lay astern of the lightship on the end of a light line. Still the aircraft would not leave them alone, machine-gunning into the water close by. Mr George, reasoning that the Germans wished them to abandon the lightship altogether, cut the line. This action marked the beginning for the crew of a most savage test of endurance.

They decided to try to make the coast in the area of The Wash, 25 miles away to the west. Mr George, who had been a trawler skipper during the First World War, knew his business and the crew were confident of reaching the shore safely. The men set the dipping lug-sail on their tiny red craft, a 16-foot clinker-built dinghy. With a man on the tiller and four others manning the oars, they bent to their task.

Just days before, London had recorded its coldest January day since 1881. The reason for the protracted cold spell was a fierce south-easterly wind blowing across the North Sea from continental Europe, itself in the grip of a major freeze. Holland was having its coldest January for 100 years and its inland waterway system was iced to a standstill. Far out from the west coast of Jutland, the sea was frozen solid. Between the isle of Romo and the mainland, people were driving cars on the ice. There were ice floes in the River Seine at Paris.

Laced by this bitter wind and soaked by spray, the lightship crew slowly became numb and their strength began to wane. All the while they were being driven north, away from their hoped-for landfall. Throughout that day they sailed and rowed and baled the super-chilled water out of the boat, then deep into the night, suffering agonies from the relentless cold. By 2.30 am they were close to the shore. Only two men were still able to row, the rest barely alive. Now they heard breakers. As they approached the beach – so near yet, oh so far – the boat struck a sandbar, capsized and threw the men into the pounding surf.

Just one man reached the shore alive, 30-year-old Jack Sanders, a strong, fit man and a very capable swimmer. His home was in Great Yarmouth, 40 miles south of where he now found himself. But not safety, not warmth, not security awaited Sanders on that black morning. The wind-swept beach was quite deserted. How long he lay there he could not remember but he recovered sufficiently to begin to drag himself away from the water's edge and managed to keep going until the bulk of a building loomed before him. It seemed to be a holiday hut or shed. With the last of his strength, Sanders pulled himself inside. There, he found some old sacking and wrapped them round his freezing body. At first light, he set himself to find some habitation and managed to walk to the nearest village, Mablethorpe.

LV 61 was eventually towed into Yarmouth where she was visited by the Duke of Kent. He was escorted round the ship by a lifelong friend of Jack Sanders, W.H. 'Wally' Pulfer. Mr Pulfer was himself a survivor from the lightship tender THV *Reculver* which was bombed and sunk on January 9th after supplying stores to the *Cockle* Lightship, some of whose crew were aboard *Reculver* and among the 50 injured in the attack. Clearly, the Duke was looking for damage but except for a little splintering on a rail there was nothing.

Jack Sanders joined the Royal Navy and was a Chief Petty Officer coxswain on destroyers. After the war he became boatswain of the Trinity House vessel *Warden*. Described by Wally Pulfer as 'a fine seaman' – the ultimate accolade for those who made their living from the sea – Jack Sanders died in 1959.

The attacks on the lightships caused outrage. German communiques at the time made a point of referring to the light vessels as 'armed outpost ships'. This was completely untrue. But if the Transport and General Workers Union in Britain had had their way, the lightships would have been armed immediately after the *East Dudgeon* affair.

The then General Secretary, Ernest Bevin, a member of the War Cabinet, wrote to the Admiralty and to the lighthouse authority, the Elder Brethren of Trinity House, requesting some means of self-defence for the crews. He cited the case of one of his members, Seaman Bardolfe Boulton, recently transferred from the Royal Naval Volunteer Reserve to Trinity House to serve on lightships. Seaman Boulton was one of the ill-fated crew of the *East Dudgeon*. Like Wally Pulfer, he had just survived the sinking of the *THV Reculver*.

The lightships were not immediately armed. Instead they were gradually withdrawn. At one point in 1941, there were just two left on the east coast – at the Cork station off Harwich and at the Humber station in the mouth of that river. This situation did not last for long and the lightships began to reappear, this time fitted with guns. The weaponry was not standardised across the light vessel fleet. Anti-aircraft guns were usually of the Hotchkiss or Oerlikon type, their crews protected by armoured shields. Lewis machine guns or Marlin machine guns were

Seaman Bardolfe Boulton (centre) of the *LV 61* (*East Dudgeon*).

also carried. These weapons were not usually mounted but hand-held, their weight supported by leaning the barrels on a rail.

An inventory of armaments aboard *LV 90* on February 12th, 1942 showed the equipment as: two Hotchkiss anti-aircraft guns with 1245 rounds of ammunition and two Lewis guns with 1471 rounds. Typically, lightships underwent stability tests which resulted in about 15 tons of added ballast to compensate for the weight of the armament on deck. Navy ratings normally manned the weapons. Four extra ratings for the *Humber* Lightship were expected 'to find their own bedding and mess gear and do their own cooking'.

The only light vessel deployed in Scotland during the war, the *North Carr*, had its own crew trained in the use of their Oerlikon and Lewis guns at the shore-based gunnery school, *HMS Claverhouse*, and at the firing range at Longniddry, East Lothian. These weapons were never fired in anger.

Footnote: Did the Royal Air Force ever attack a lightship? The answer is yes – and no. During their occupation of the Low Countries, the Germans converted Dutch Lightship No 9 into an air defence vessel at Wemeldinge off the Dutch coast. While engaged in this role the ship was sunk in 1942 by bombers of the RAF. No. 9 was raised in 1946, restored to lightship duties again and served until 1979 when she was sold.

The *Dudgeon Shoal* Lightship station was the second ever in the world and the first to be sited in the open sea. It was established in 1736 about 25 miles north of Cromer, Norfolk. The aim was to allow the safer passage of colliers and other traders between Spurn Point off the north edge of the Humber estuary, and the north Norfolk coast. Despite being held by two anchors the *Dudgeon Shoal* Lightship was blown off station several times. All the earliest light vessels had attending vessels stationed in the nearest port. After every gale these ships were sent out to check on their lightships and reposition them if necessary. All carried new mooring ropes and anchors. They were often needed.

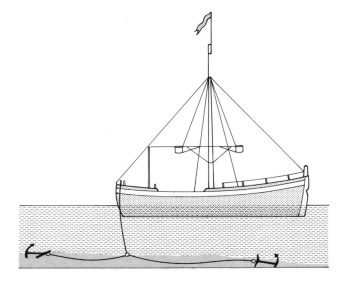

The mooring system of an early Dudgeon ship. Redrawn from *Der Bundesminister für Verkehr*, Bonn 1965.

LIGHT BITES

A crewman of the *Cork* light vessel off Harwich spotted a small yacht astern of the ship. The sails were furled and the sole occupant was rowing hard, barely managing to stem the tide. The lightsman hailed the yachtsman who shouted back, 'I'm lost. Just keep going and I'll follow you into harbour!'

Towards the end of the 19th century, attempts to link lightships with the shore by telegraph cable met with limited success. In 1887 a cable nine miles long was laid to the *Sunk* Lightship in the north-eastern approaches to the Thames but it constantly fouled the mooring cable. Although these efforts continued, the real answer – radio – was just around the corner. The first ever emergency wireless message sent by a ship at sea came from the *East Goodwin* Lightship in 1899. In dense fog on April 28th that year, the schooner-rigged steamship *R.F. Mathews* ran into the lightship, badly damaging her bows. Master of the lightship, Captain Clayson, sent a Morse message to this effect to the South Foreland lighthouse 12 miles away, using the spark-gap transmitter on board. The link was set up with help from 'that chap Marconi.' Captain Clayson was able to give a detailed report of the damage and requested that another lightship be dispatched immediately to relieve his ship. By 1911 seven light vessels, including all four marking the Goodwin Sands, were fitted with radio apparatus.

In 1977, the Sea Cadet Commanding Officer whose base was a former lightship at Norwich was relieved to get an offer from the Haven Ports Yacht Club at Levington Marina near Felixstowe to remove his ship's lantern free of charge so that it could be used in their own lightship clubhouse. Some of the sea cadets had been climbing to the lantern to get a good view into the bedrooms of a nearby hotel.

An extract from the 1843 list of stores of the *North-west* Lightship (launched as *The Prince*) at the mouth of the River Mersey included the following item: 1,336 wicks for oil lamps which burned 'only the best' winter-strained sperm whale oil.

LV North Carr

*D*uring the early part of December, 1959, the east coast of Scotland was being battered by the worst gales in 22 years. By the time daylight faded on Monday the 7th, several ships had been sunk or wrecked that month and 14 seamen and two Coastguard officers had lost their lives. There were just two manned lightships in Scottish waters, ten miles apart. The *Abertay* was in the Tay estuary while the North Carr station, off Fife Ness at the northern entrance to the Forth, marked the deadly North Carr rocks and the reef that ran inshore from that point.

As the elements conducted their pointless argument all around him, Master of the *North Carr*, George Rosie, may have had cause to recall a battle of a different kind, also witnessed by the ship. The date was October 16th, 1939, the time 3 pm. As the *North Carr* lay quietly at anchor, nine German bombers, Junkers 88s of I Wing, KG 30 based more than 400 miles away at Westerland on the island of Sylt, swept over the ship at masthead height, the swastikas looming large on their wings and fuselage. Their aim was to attack the Forth Bridge and naval units in the river.

As the lightship crew watched from their ringside seats the bombers were intercepted by Spitfires from 602 (City of Glasgow) and 603 (City of Edinburgh) Squadrons. One bomber was shot down about two miles to the seaward side of the ship and one other off Port Seton. The German raid, the first on mainland Britain of the Second World War, was not a total failure however and three Royal Navy vessels were damaged. The bridge was not hit.

The *North Carr* was withdrawn from her station on July 5th, 1940 and placed in the west end of the Old Dock, Leith. Even here she could not escape the attentions of the Luftwaffe. During an air raid on the docks that summer, a length of railway track blown into the air by a bomb blast fell, point first, on the lightship's upper deck. In her present berth in Victoria Dock, Dundee, the mark from that impact on the starboard side near the charthouse can still be seen.

The *North Carr* was acquired by the Admiralty in April, 1942 and having been towed through the Caledonian Canal under the command of her Master A.K. Walker, served for three years in the outer reaches of the Firth of Clyde, initially 14 miles south-west of Ailsa Craig. She was anchored in 60 fathoms, probably the

The *North Carr* lightship.
Photograph courtesy of Dr. Alec Wattison M.B.C.R.B.

deepest water ever experienced by a British lightship. Even the *Seven Stones* off the Scilly Isles, the only genuine Atlantic lightship operating in British waters, had only 40 fathoms beneath her keel. The Scottish crewmen immediately noticed a more comfortable motion about their ship compared to the more confused action at her usual east coast anchorage in just 22 fathoms.

Her light characteristic had been changed on the advice of Northern Lighthouse Board engineer John Oswald, who had studied the lights in the immediate vicinity. The ship's familiar two flashes of white every 30 seconds became two red flashes every 30 seconds. As often happened in wartime, no attempt was made to have the red match the range of the white and the effective candlepower was cut from 500,000 to 200,000.

In what must have led to a degree of uncertainty, the *North Carr* was referred to in all radio communications as 'The Clyde Light Vessel' although still bearing her own name on her sides. Her task was to act as a marker through a minefield for the Atlantic convoys. Her hull had been painted grey and degaussed or 'wiped' to save her from magnetic mines. But the real enemy was convoy shipping. She was hit twice, on one of these occasions by the liner *Franconia* then acting as a troopship. Had this been anything other than a glancing blow, the *North Carr* story would have ended right there. To lessen the chances of this happening the ship was moved further along the swept channel.

The first lightship ever to be equipped with AWD (acoustic warning device) to detect the presence of aircraft, the *North Carr* was right in the front line. Her confidential papers were kept permanently between two lead sheets, ready for ditching over the side in the event of her being boarded by enemy forces. A close encounter with the *Kriegsmarine* duly ensued.

During a raid on a convoy on January 15th, 1945, the German submarine U-482 (Kapitanleutnant Hartmut von Matuschka) torpedoed the Norwegian tanker *Spinanger* near the lightship. With three crewmen dead on board, the badly-damaged tanker was beached in Kames Bay. Next day U-482 was detected underneath or very close to the lightship. The raider was destroyed by ships of the 2nd Escort Group, including the 1480-ton sloop *HMS Amethyst*, which was to achieve fame in the summer of 1949 as the warship which ran the gauntlet of Chinese Communist artillery down the Yangtze River from Chinkiang to the sea.

The *North Carr's* most tragic and dramatic moment however, was to be reserved for peacetime and the storm of 1959. As the two Scottish lightships bucked and heaved that night, disaster was just hours away. The gale was blowing from the worst possible quarter – the south-east. For days, an incalculable weight of water had been shouldered all the way across the North Sea from Germany. By the time the waves dashed themselves to pieces on the Scottish coastline they were 40 feet high with a huge spread between the crests, details measured as a matter of course by an interferometer in the *North Carr's* radio room and due for eventual dispatch to the oceanography unit at Bracknell, Berkshire.

The *North Carr's* light was precisely the same height – 40 feet – above sea level. The electrically-powered light was designed to be independent of the motion of the ship. Suspended on two sets of gimbals and weighted by a brass pendulum to keep it upright, the idea was to have the beam from the light always parallel to the horizon despite the movement of the vessel. On rare occasions, in most extreme weather, the light would be 'braked' to avoid possible collision with any part of the lantern itself. So it was that night and the white pencil of the light sketched an endless series of crazy patterns, now in the black sky, now in the angry sea.

The *North Carr's* mooring system was that of a typical light vessel. The single anchor was a stockless type weighing three tons, the absence of the stock at right angles to the main arm of the anchor enabling it to be raised deep into the hawse-pipe. The riding cable consisted of 255 fathoms (about 500 metres) of 1⅝-inch stud link chain, the stud or bar across the centre of each link helping to prevent it from elongating under exactly the kind of pressure now being exerted. It was designed to hold a ship three times the weight of the 250-ton *North Carr*.

Joining the anchor to the main cable was a three-fathom length of two-inch open link chain. The cable was divided into lengths of 15 fathoms, each length joined to its neighbour by a clenched cable shackle. Also, at regular spaces, four swivels reduced the chance of the cable knotting or kinking. The most vulnerable point – where it left the ship – was called 'the nip'. Here a length of canvas was wrapped around the chain to reduce wear upon it. Despite the immense strength inherent in the system, at two minutes past two o'clock in the morning the cable parted.

At that exact same moment a despairing radio message was being sent out from a doomed ship. The voice of the operator aboard the Norwegian freighter *Elfreida* spoke the last words heard by any of the crew of 20: 'We are going down. Thank you for all your help. We are getting out our starboard lifeboat and will try to leave the ship.' The *Elfreida* was found the following day, upside down, 100 miles west of Stavanger.

Unaware of the disaster unfolding 250 miles away to the north-east, the helpless lightship began to drift, often turning beam on to the full weight of the storm and being pushed almost onto her side. These were the conditions under which George Rosie's crew had to try to drop the first of their two emergency or bower anchors.

They did not have much time. Their correct station was already close to the shore and now they were being driven at an angle towards it. Here, luck may have played a vital part. Although they could not know it, the cable had parted close to the anchor. One of the two-inch links had given way, leaving about 12 tons of chain in the water, much of it dragging along the seabed. Undoubtedly it slowed the rate of drift, buying some precious time. The crew worked quickly and well. At 2.50 am the spare anchor cable on the port side rattled out, the 1⅓-ton anchor biting and holding the ship. She was now riding to about 90 fathoms of emergency chain.

The 2" link in the ground tackle chain which parted and first set the *North Carr* adrift.

In the Coastguard station at Fife Ness, Bruce Burgess had spotted the lightship moving off station. He and his colleague Charlie Jones telephoned Coastguard District Officer Joe Levitt and the first steps to mount a rescue got under way. The lifeboat at nearby Anstruther would normally have been launched but the tide was out and conditions in the harbour mouth were quite impossible. The lifeboat station at Arbroath reported a similar situation but at Broughty Ferry, deep inside the River Tay, the lifeboat *Mona* was capable of launching at any state of the tide. She prepared for the run down her long slipway.

The *Mona* was a veteran of many rescues. A Watson cabin-type lifeboat, she was strong and reliable. Weighing close to 20 tons, her hull consisted of a double skin of mahogany over a framework of Canadian rock elm, with both stem and stern posts of English oak. For buoyancy and safety she was equipped with 142 air-cases and was divided into seven watertight compartments. Her twin screws were powered by two 40 hp engines, both of which were themselves watertight. She could travel 116 miles without refuelling at her top speed of 8.5 knots. At a pinch, she could cram 95 people aboard.

By 3.13 am the crew of eight were aboard inside the lifeboat shed. The doors swung open and the *Mona* thundered down the greased track of the slipway. She dug her nose in, porpoised upwards and settled down to her dangerous trip. She had about 25 miles to cover to reach the *North Carr*, including the notorious bar across the Tay estuary. The weather she had to contend with would have been hazardous in daylight. In the pitch black of that awful night, the risks were frightful. At 3.36 am Charlie Jones called the lifeboat with the message: '*North Carr* is on the air now.'

The *Mona* could not raise the lightship and Jones called again saying: '*North Carr* has just fired a rocket. Did you see it?' The lifeboat replied that she had not and asked for the position of the lightship. They were told the *North Carr* was riding to a spare anchor two miles north by west of Fife Ness and was firing rockets at regular intervals.

At Buddon Ness on the north side of the mouth of the Tay, Senior Coastguard David Mearns saw the *Mona* as she cleared the Ness about 4 am and six minutes later the lifeboat reported herself abeam of the *Abertay* Lightship. The lightship crew, skippered by John Gillies, could see nothing of the *Mona* from their position at sea level, despite keeping a close lookout. Gillies described the waves pounding his ship 'as big as three-storey blocks of flats'.

But from his elevated vantage point, Mearns was able to observe the *Mona* turn south into St Andrews Bay as the *North Carr* fired another rocket. Asked if they had seen it, the *Mona's* radio operator was only able to gasp: 'No... our position... we have just passed the middle buoy on the bar and we are just hanging on.' At 4.48 am, in response to another request from base about the latest *North Carr* rocket, the *Mona's* final message was: 'Yes. We saw that one. We have cleared the bar.'

The *North Carr* had been trying to contact the *Mona* by radio but encountered only a frustrating crackle. The Master resorted to putting out the following call several times: 'If you can hear us but cannot respond, please fire a rocket.' Nothing happened.

Further attempts to raise the lifeboat failed but Fife Ness coastguards reported seeing her masthead light in St Andrews Bay at 5.39 am. (It could only have been the *Mona*. No other vessel except the *North Carr* was in the bay that night).

Jones signalled the lightship: 'Do you see the ship's lights approaching you now, bearing 332° Fife Ness?'

The lightship replied: 'Yes, I think it is the lifeboat. Will burn another flare.' The approaching lights vanished shortly after.

The trauma for the *North Carr* crew was about to enter a new phase. At 6.30 am

The aftermath of disaster. The Broughty Ferry lifeboat *Mona* lies forlornly on the beach.
Photograph courtesy of D.C. Thomson & Co. Limited, Dundee.

her emergency cable parted at the compressor on deck and she was again at the mercy of the storm. The men took just 15 minutes to get their starboard – and last – spare anchor into the sea and Captain Rosie began gradually to pay out its cable until a full 140 fathoms was in the water.

Rosie also let go about 100 fathoms of cable from the main mooring tier in his chain locker to help hold the ship and to lighten the bow, making it easier for the *North Carr* to ride the storm. By this time the lightship was roughly a mile from the rocky beach at Babbet Ness near the village of Boarhills. For the moment at least, she was holding.

With the first grey light of morning one of the great tragedies in the history of the lifeboat service revealed itself to a stunned nation. On the beach at Buddon Ness, a man walking his dog found the *Mona* rocking to and fro in the surf. A single red navigation light still glowed from the bow. Most of her dead crew were inside. It may have been fitting that the first man to board the *Mona* was David Mearns.

In the course of 24 years of service with the RNLI, the *Mona* had saved 118 lives, nine of those from the steam trawler *Quixotic* almost exactly 20 years before. For that rescue, the then coxswain, James Coull, was awarded the RNLI's silver medal with bronze medals going to motor mechanic John Grieve and acting second coxswain George B. Smith. The latter two were on board during the *Mona's* heroic effort to reach the *North Carr*.

The loss of the *Mona* and her crew had deep personal echoes for Mearns. He had been in command of the *Abertay* Lightship during a fierce storm in January, 1937 when his ship was driven right across the main channel leading into the Tay, effectively closing the port of Dundee. He and his men were taken off by the *Mona* and landed at Broughty Ferry. (See *The Abertay Lightship 1877–1939*.)

As the lifeboat had been conducting her final, fatal duel with the elements, two other ships were making ready for sea. In Granton Harbour, the lighthouse tender

Taken in calmer, if foggy weather, this view of the *North Carr* was captured from the lighthouse tender *Pharos*.

Pharos (Captain J.W. Hunter) had to endure a frustrating delay until the flood tide had produced sufficient water in the harbour entrance to allow her to leave safely. Deeper into the Forth, at Rosyth Naval Base, the Admiralty tug *Earner* had also been recruited to attend the stricken lightship. The *Pharos* finally got under way at 8.15 am and reached the *North Carr* at noon to find the wind east by south-east force 8/9 with a massive swell running. The *Earner* arrived about an hour later. The tug began a seemingly endless series of attempts to get a line aboard the lightship.

Captain Hunter was gravely concerned for the beleaguered crew and although it was plainly impossible to launch a boat from the *North Carr*, consideration was given to have them leave the ship on one of the inflatable rafts stored on deck. This option was abandoned in favour of the lesser evil of leaving the men on board until the following day. Lightship crewman Tom Henderson, later to became assistant Master of the *North Carr*, remembers the discussion.

'We felt we could never have survived in those conditions,' he said.

'I recall pointing to the lantern and saying: *If the worst comes to the worst, that will do for me.*'

Captain Rosie now ordered his crew to manhandle a 5 cwt (254 kg) kedge anchor from its berth near the stern all the way along the port side, shackle it to the remains of the port anchor cable and get the makeshift rig over the side. The effort required to heave an anchor weighing a quarter of a ton along a pitching, heaving deck was a strength-sapping experience for the already tired men, but by 10.30 pm the job was done. Now they could only wait out the night, deeply conscious of the fact that their ship was in shallow water and every plunge into the trough of a wave placed her keel within a few feet of the seabed. Both the *Pharos* and the *Earner* stood by, the *North Carr's* position constantly monitored by radar during the hours of darkness.

Next day the gale ranted on with undiminished fury and further attempts to secure a connection between lightship and tug only met with further frustrating failure. When the *Earner* finally ran out of line-firing rockets, the last chance of getting the lightship in tow disappeared. It was now midday. Captain Hunter, after consulting with George Rosie, decided to call in rescue helicopters from RAF Leuchars seven miles away.

Two Bristol Sycamore machines from 228 Squadron, Coastal Command, were sent out. Tiny compared to the helicopters used in rescue work today, their mission was a daunting one. It was carried out with clinical efficiency under the command of Flight Lieutenant J.E. McCrea. An initial attempt to deposit one of the helicopter crewmen, Flight Lieutenant S. Moreau, on board the *North Carr* was abandoned as too dangerous. His mission would have been to familiarise the lightship crew with the rescue harness. In three trips beginning at 12.30 pm the helicopters lifted off the crew one by one from the roof of the charthouse. The men were landed in a field about four miles south of St Andrews. The entire operation was concluded by 1.27 pm.

The storm-blurred images of the *North Carr* rescue somehow heighten the sense of drama as one crewman makes his perilous ascent to the helicopter.

In the words of RAF Master Navigator Scoggins:

'We got them all off without a bump or a splash. They looked unshaven and tired but were quite cheery. I don't suppose any of them had ever been in a helicopter before and it must have been quite an undertaking for them after all they had been through. These men must be afraid of nothing.'

Sergeant George Britton, navigator on the second helicopter said flying conditions had been appalling.

'The most terrifying thing was the lantern on the ship which was lifting and dropping with the waves, making it extremely difficult to drop the line at the right time. When we did manage it, the men had to fix on the harness quickly to allow us to steer clear of the light.'

In one heart-stopping moment the spinning blades of a helicopter came within an estimated five feet of the lantern. The rescue had been watched by knots of silent people who had gathered at various vantage points along the shore.

On the Friday, although the weather was still bad, some of the reserve crew of the lightship, plus Captain Rosie, went on board and the ship was towed into Leith, her last life-saving anchor and cable having had to be left in the sea. The only damage, apart from the lost moorings, was to the main mast at the stern. One of the aircraft had dropped a leather wallet containing a note onto the lightship, asking the crew to cut it down to enable the rescuers to get in closer.

The crew of the *North Carr* lightship in the Golf Hotel, Crail after rescue by helicopter, 10th December, 1959. George Rosie (right), Tom Henderson just behind.

One of the crews of the early *North Carr* lightship.
From Scottish Ethnological Archive, National Museums of Scotland.

The first purpose-built *North Carr* Lightship went on station on July 27th, 1889, replacing a temporary vessel.* Her wooden hull and frame were of teak and oak with the bottom planking of English elm. In 1895 a complaint was made to her owners, the Commissioners of Northern Lights, that her fixed white light was not distinctive enough. In an interesting reply, lighthouse engineer D.A. Stevenson, grandson of the great Robert Stevenson, remarked: 'The *North Carr* vessel is essentially a fog signal ship, not a light vessel, the light being more for preventing the vessel itself from being run into'.

Nonetheless in 1910, as a result of continued complaints, the ship was put on the slipway at Granton, Edinburgh and upgraded. Its light characteristic was changed to alternate red and green and the fuel switched from oil to acetylene gas, which was produced on board. A new and far more powerful motor siren, worked by compressed air, replaced the original signal.

For the crew, life was hard. The vessel was rather low-slung and shipped a lot of water. Facilities were described by a former crewman as 'hopeless', the men having to wash in buckets. The ship never had radio right up to the time she was replaced by a steel vessel in 1933, communication with the Fife Ness Coastguard service was by signal flags. The limitations of this ludicrous practice meant that the main means of dealing with emergencies to the ship or to crew members was to pray that they did not happen.

George Rosie, later to become Master of the new ship, remembers the old *North Carr* as a 'smelly ship' – possibly a consequence of the chemical reaction between the wood of her two skins, the salt poured in between and the water which inevitably seeped into the gaps. There were two bronze cannons on board for firing shots to warn vessels which were standing into danger. A ramrod and gunpowder were provided. The guns were only fired once or twice and were considered by crewmen too dangerous to use. They were mounted on wooden bogeys and held down by leather straps.

For all her disadvantages, the ship was a priceless asset to the great volume of maritime traffic which tramped along the east coast of Scotland prior to the Second World War and for that reason alone she could fairly claim to be a more important vessel than her successor which had much less 'passing trade'. Also the quality of the service she offered was higher since the vessels she kept away from the North Carr reef had none of the sophisticated post-war equipment available for navigating in treacherous conditions.

The old *North Carr* was sold for £275 at the end of her 44-year working life to shipbreaker Harold Hinks of Appledore, Devon. Much of the timber went into houses being built in Appledore. Some of these houses overlook the sea.

*The Courier and Advertiser of November 7th, 1975 carried a tale which has now survived for more than a century in the village of Kingsbarns, a few miles from where the temporary ship was sited. One night, according to the report, the foghorn was working from dusk until after dawn. Local farmer Jimmy Brown received a complaint in the morning that his cow had been bellowing all night and had kept awake the occupants of the local mansion house. The foghorn was thereafter known as 'Jimmy Broon's coo'.

The Case for Power

Many a debate raged over the latter history of the lightship service worldwide on whether or not to equip the ships with propulsion engines. Most Western countries produced some powered lightships without abandoning completely the 'dumb ship' principle and it was commonplace to have a mix of powered and dumb vessels in service at the same time, the self-drive vessels usually at those anchorages subject to the greatest stresses.

Many countries went over completely to power, progressing gradually towards this goal. The Americans produced their first powered lightships in 1891. The advice given in 1915 to light vessel masters by the U.S. Lighthouse Bureau concerning the use of engines in the manoeuvre known as 'steaming up to the moorings' was contained in Instruction No. 255:

> *Use of propelling power – the utmost caution and judgement should be exercised by the commanding officer in stormy weather of the propelling machinery while riding at the moorings and if found necessary, the speed should be carefully controlled by the engineer officer who shall be in communication with the commanding officer at all times.*

Vessels with drive units were more expensive to build and to run and needed better qualified crews. Even in the Soviet Union however, where the state wallet for non-military projects was more or less welded shut, two lightships with 300 hp engines were ordered from the shipyard at Turku, Finland in 1961 for working in that huge salt lake, the Caspian Sea.

Yet in Britain, home of the lightship, every vessel ever built was a dumb ship, having to be towed everywhere it needed to go. Port authorities and harbour boards in Britain occasionally ordered their own lightships and slavishly followed the same pattern.

Even the last generation of British lightships, built at the end of the 1960s, had no drive machinery and it is a supreme irony that the crews of British lightships of the 19th century had more chance of helping themselves in emergencies than their counterparts 100 years later – they had storm sails which, in optimum conditions, could even be used to get the ship on or off station.

A further irony lies in the well-documented reluctance of The Elder Brethren of Trinity House to accept the lightship principle in the first place because of the difficulty of keeping the ships on station.

The *North Carr* episode presented possibly the definitive case for propulsion power. Here was a ship which could have used her engine, if only she had one, to reduce the load on her cable. The chances are the ship would not have broken free. If she had, the engine would have supplied the instant opportunity to steer. If it had been necessary to deploy a second anchor, that cable in turn would have had a better chance to hold. Most important of all, it is inconceivable that a lifeboat would have been launched on such a night had the lightship been able to manoeuvre.

One of many examples of a lightship getting itself out of trouble is that of the *Diamond Shoal* ship at Cape Hatteras, North Carolina, on America's Atlantic coast. Driven off station during a hurricane in September, 1933, she dragged her 2½-ton anchor for five miles until she entered the breakers at the Cape. Only then did the captain reluctantly slip his moorings and use his motor to guide the ship away from danger. The ship received a tremendous battering and both skipper and mate were badly injured. For their devotion to duty President Franklin D. Roosevelt presented the crew with a framed letter of commendation.

Engines on lightships offered no guarantee of safety. Many vessels so equipped have still come to grief. And not every lightship skipper believed in 'steaming up to the moorings'. A few worried about steaming beyond the moorings, inadvertently placing their ship in danger. Yet it's impossible to ignore the edge the engines gave in safety terms, both for the crews and for other mariners in a number of ways. Tending less to break loose or drag, the powered ship had a greater likelihood of maintaining its presence exactly where it should be in rough weather. It was less dependent upon rescue services, which often had to be called to unpowered lightships in desperately dangerous conditions and the powered lightship was itself able to participate in rescues.

Advocates of the 'dumb ship' principle made much of the system of reserve anchors. This was essential equipment for any lightship, powered or not. But in the conditions when they were most likely to be needed, they could not hope to match the strength of a main cable system which had failed, even though veered out to its maximum length. Reserve anchors were much smaller – typically half the weight of the primary anchor – and their cables shorter. Thus the angle between ship and spare anchor on the seabed would be more acute, placing yet greater strain on it than the cable which had already failed.

It was also standard practice for the seabed to be surveyed before a lightship was sited, to ensure its suitability for holding the ship. A back-up mooring, used in circumstances when it would come under intense pressure, had also to absorb an initial shock not placed upon the main cable and must hit the seabed at random, perhaps on ground wholly unsuited to good grip.

Despite first-class mooring equipment, light vessels around the British coast have been pushed off station hundreds of times, mostly through dragging their anchors, since the time when it became practical to build these ships with motive power. The argument that powered ships would have had to be built bigger is not just lame. It isn't true. Many countries produced such vessels which were smaller than, or roughly the same size as, the biggest British lightships – and not just for sheltered anchorages such as in rivers.

The temptation is to believe there was at work a penny pinching culture embedded deep in the decision-making process of the lighthouse services which even extended to ships' lifeboats. Crews were expected to propel themselves into stormy waters in boats which had no means of movement other than by oar or sail – just as they had done when the lightship service began in the 18th century.

In the absence of manned lightships these days, the points made no longer have any practical application and are therefore academic. But it seems extraordinary that in Britain, where such wonderful work was done to lead the world in the development of floating lights, the periodic calls for powered lightships were always dismissed.

Author's note: In the service of fairness I feel it proper to declare a personal interest in the North Carr episode.

I was raised in Broughty Ferry. At the age of seven I learned to swim off the lifeboat slipway. The sight of the boat thundering down that long slip never failed to raise the hair on the back of my neck. Often I would climb the steps to the door of the lifeboat shed and if it was open I'd go in.

What I found there remains one of the sharpest and most poignant of my childhood memories. There she stood, immense in that confined space, immaculate in her blue, red and white RNLI livery. Brasswork gleamed dully in the subdued light.

The quiet was cathedral-like but even at so tender an age the sense poured in that although this was her home, it was not her element. She was a creature of the storm. What dangerous waters that keel had torn through! What relief beyond description the sight of her inspired in many a despairing heart!

This was a force for good, nothing else.

The Mona has been gone for many years. Shortly after her tragic rescue attempt she was deliberately destroyed by fire in an act which provoked outrage at the time. Even the lifeboat shed no longer houses the present lifeboat which nowadays is kept permanently in the water.

The crew of the Mona are gone too but certainly not forgotten. I knew most of them, one in particular, John Grieve. He was just 22 when he died that night in 1959.

33 years after the Mona disaster I became manager of the North Carr Lightship Maritime Museum when the ship was based at Anstruther in Fife. During my three years with the North Carr I formed an affection for her that will never fade with time. She, too, existed to serve and preserve.

I may be the only person alive with such strong emotional ties to both vessels and it is possible that in my assessment of the need for engines on lightships, some of this has crept in to colour what ought to be a wholly detached view. I do not believe so but I cannot in all conscience vouch for it.

The Channel
Rock Lightship

*L*ife for the lightship crewman was a curious cocktail of danger and deep bore-dom. Aboard an Australian lightship towards the end of the 19th century, this may have been doubly true. The Department of Harbours and Marine for the colony of Queensland – the Commonwealth of Australia was not formed until 1901, when the colonies were designated states – reported that by 1894 the *Proudfoot Shoal* Lightship had been at her moorings without relief since the light station was established in 1883, a period of 11 years.

The report ran on:

Experience proved that the loneliness of the life aboard this ship had a depressing effect on the spirits of the crew and it was decided in future not to keep the men for more than 12 months in that vessel without relief.

The *Proudfoot Shoal* ship occupied probably the most isolated anchorage of any light vessel throughout the entire span of the service worldwide. Her task was to mark an undersea hill that soared abruptly from the Arafura Shelf to a point just nine feet below the surface. She rode to her moorings in the Arafura Sea (a somewhat altered environment from the parched desert it had been during the last Ice Age) in the western Pacific 90 kilometres west of Thursday Island in the Torres Strait, that treacherous gateway for ships voyaging from the teeming ports of Asia to the south Pacific, the eastern ports of Austalia and New Zealand.

She was supplied monthly, usually by the steamer *Albatross* which was based on the island, itself parted from civilisation by the prodigious distances of the north Australian continent. It was still very much a land of scattered pioneers and Aborigines who had crossed from New Guinea at least 50,000 years ago, either sailing from island to island or, before that time, via the land bridge whose remnants are the Torres Strait islands.

Stuck deep in the tropics in latitude 10° 32' south and longitude 141° 28' east, the *Proudfoot Shoal* ship must have seemed to her crew a kind of floating Devil's

Island. In a very real sense, they *were* in prison, the confines of their sweltering cage the walls of the vessel itself. Indeed, it was not uncommon for lightship crews to talk of their term of duty as 'doing a stretch'.

Samuel Taylor Coleridge's immortal words from *The Ancient Mariner – As idle as a painted ship upon a painted ocean –* might have been written with the *Proudfoot Shoal* Lightship in mind.

And to relieve that idleness, what could they do? Not take a relaxing swim, certainly. The clear blue beckoning water was alive with sharks. And to remove any temptation completely, this was also home to the seasnakes that would bask in packs on the sparkling surface of the sea and to the most virulent forms of the box jellyfish, *Chironex* and *Chiropsalmus.* One brief contact with either could induce death within four minutes.

The nearest land mass was 100 kilometres to the south-east. And what a land! Australia's Cape York Peninsula was barely-explored territory, much of it dense jungle ruled by venomous snakes and insects and criss-crossed by rivers along which cruised the biggest crocodiles in the world – the dreaded 'salties'. The area also grew spear grass, a potentially lethal plant containing within each leaf a toxic, hypodermic -style point. Even today, the 54,000 square miles of the peninsula is held for the human species by just 14,000 souls.

The *Channel Rock* lightship moored at Cooktown.

In 1895, the problems of carrying out major repairs to such a remote light vessel as *Proudfoot Shoal* were highlighted by the decision to alter its light characteristic from an occulting system to a fixed beam because the clockwork mechanism for operating it had become worn and unreliable. Its task had been to lower and raise a brass cylinder over the glass chimney of the lamp, rather after the fashion of an eyelid, periodically obscuring or 'occulting' the light. In any occulting system the period of darkness was less than or equal to, that of light. The alteration to the ship's light was a matter of necessity, not preference.

In 1896 the *Proudfoot Shoal* was finally taken in tow against the prevailing easterlies for the 900 kilometre voyage to Cooktown for much-needed repairs, to be replaced by the relief vessel always kept there.

In 1904, in the face of considerable opposition, the light station was discontinued. The reason given – that the Booby Island light 40 kilometres away provided adequate cover for the shoal – was particularly weak. The 37-metre high Booby Island light had been operating for 14 years and the sudden discovery that it could also cover the *Proudfoot Shoal* manifestly had more to do with economics than with safety at sea. *Proudfoot* was very close to the edge of Booby Island's range and in anything but perfect conditions the light could not have been seen.

The shipowners who raised such a fuss had an excellent case. The Queensland coast was so poorly lit that vessels closing the Torres Strait at night always anchored and waited for daylight before tackling that dangerous passage. Although the practice of waiting for daylight was not uncommon in those days, this situation lasted in the case of the Torres Strait until the 1920s. The clear case was for more lights, not fewer.

In Queensland, the year of 1898 had seen some severe storms and 1899 was continuing in the same vein. That final year of the century had begun badly for the Harbours and Marine Department. On January 27th, their tender vessel *Dudley* made her usual trip from the port of Bowen to the Dent Island lighthouse with stores. Having unloaded she left the lighthouse in deteriorating weather, intending to seek shelter 20 kilometres to the north in the harbour at Cid Island. She never got there. A cyclone struck the area and the *Dudley* vanished without trace.

The *Channel Rock* Lightship, west of Pipon Island – sometimes known as the *Pipon Island* Lightship for that reason – and three kilometres off the boulder-buttressed Cape Melville, was sited much further north and had missed the cyclone. But the mother of all monsters was waiting in the wings – cyclone Mahina. A misnomer this, if ever there was one – a gentle breeze of a name, customarily applied to South Sea island girls noted for their grace and beauty. The very worst of luck decreed that she would have an equally potent ally.

The first hint of trouble came from the Postmaster, Mr H.P. Beach, far to the north on Thursday Island. He reported uncommonly hot conditions on the nights of March 2nd and 3rd. In his report to his Brisbane headquarters, Mr Beach went on:

The horizon to the east was lit by lightning. The sky was black and leaden and fierce-looking.

In Brisbane the weather men were becoming increasingly aware of the looming danger and were keeping an eye on not one cyclone but two. Queensland's Chief Meteorologist was Clement Wragge. Wragge was a 'character' who had taken up his appointment on January 1st, 1887. Fed up with the apparent indifference of the Australian public to the Weather Bureau, Wragge hit upon the notion of naming cyclones after girls, choosing South Sea Island names such as Mahina and Leola, as well as celebrated warriors and politicians like Hannibal and Drake, Deakin and Barton (Australian Prime Ministers), to heighten the profile of his department. When Wragge quit in July 1903, the practice of naming cyclones went with him. It would be the early 1960s before it was resumed.

Wragge was a worried man. Mahina had already devastated the Solomon Islands and was now approaching the Queensland coast from the direction of the Louisiade Archipelago, a small chain of islands east of New Guinea. On the other side of the Cape York Peninsula in the Gulf of Carpentaria cyclone Nachon, prosaically described as a tropical disturbance, was starting to track across the land, heading erratically towards the east coast.

Wragge noted:

> 'Much indeed do we regret that we have no means of advising the Barrier Reef lightships and the pearling fleets of the approaching storm between Cooktown and the Torres Strait.'

On Saturday the 4th, in the wide expanse of Princess Charlotte Bay, more than 100 luggers of the Thursday Island mother-of-pearl shell and bêche-de-mer (sea cucumber) fleets were strung out, mostly close to their mother schooners. They had set out from the island in early February in pursuit of the lucrative undersea harvest to be had north of Cooktown. Included in this motley collection of vessels were the tiny swimming boats used by the pearl shell divers. The biggest concentration, 45, was in Bathurst Bay, at the south-eastern end of the bigger bay.

The crews had chosen to gather here to replenish their stores and gear. As it was the weekend, it was also time for time off. The men were in the habit of taking their entire families to sea with them and the atmosphere was happy and relaxed. There was an international flavour about the people of the fleets – Filipinos, Japanese, Malays, Aborigines, South Sea and Torres Strait islanders as well as a tiny number of Europeans all combined to produce a maritime community of improbable closeness.

Bathurst Bay was an idyllic spot. Bounded by the horns of Cape Melville and Bathurst Head, it was the tropical paradise of everyone's dreams. Warm blue water whispered upon beaches of white sand. Beyond the beach lay coastal heathland and low melaleuca and eucalyptus woods charmingly interrupted by the occasional palm tree. That sparkling day, the air barely stirred in the summer heat. For hundreds of those enjoying the moment, death was a few short hours away.

On board the *Channel Rock* Lightship the Master, Swedish national Gustav Oscar Fuhrman, was celebrating his 49th birthday with his three crewmen – Mate Douglas Lee and lightsmen Henry Karr and Dan Crowley. Fuhrman had been granted a coast pilot's licence for sailing vessels by the Marine Board on January 17th, 1890 but he stayed with the service for only a few months before accepting the position of Master of the *Piper Island* Lightship. His transfer 250 kilometres south to the *Channel Rock* lightship occurred in 1895 when the old *Piper Island* ship was replaced by a more modern vessel. In the fickle game of chance that is life, Fuhrman had just suffered a fatal roll of the dice.

The Channel Rock was the principal hazard to navigation in the area of Cape Melville and the presence of the lightship was designed to usher ships around it and guide them safely west of Pipon Island. The vessel was one of three marking the twisting, reef-riven Inner Route between the coast and the 2100-kilometre Great Barrier Reef, a passage described in Jeff Toghill's *Circumnavigating Australia's Coastline – A Yachtsman's Manual* as 'a nightmare for navigators even in an age of accurate charts and sophisticated equipment'.

The *Channel Rock* station was established in December, 1877 but by 1890 the ship there was in bad condition and a new wooden lightship was built at Townsville at a cost of £3943, £2000 of which went on the hull. She was 76 feet long and 16 feet in the beam, drawing four feet six inches forward and six feet aft. The ship was equipped with a dioptric light system in which the lenses collected light and condensed it into a horizontal 10° band. Her single fixed white beam, fuelled by kerosene, was of the sixth order of brightness (aids to navigation lights were graded into six orders). It was visible at a distance of 14 kilometres.

The ship took up duty in 1891 but by 1893 was already showing signs of weakness, the result, according to the Australian Maritime Safety Authority in Brisbane, of unsound timber and inferior materials used during her construction.

The Authority reported: *The decks were difficult to keep tight and one of the wooden breasthooks forward had broken away.* These were matters of the gravest concern. The breasthooks were crucial to the integrity of the bow, being large pieces of timber bolted within and across it. Even at the end of its first year in service, 45 fathoms of new chain had to be provided for the ship. This latest addition to the lightship fleet was already proving costly to maintain.

All along the Inner Route danger lurked for shipping. The channel was desperately narrow in places and survey work by *H.M.S. Dart* (Captain Parry, R.N.) was still going on. At that time many undiscovered traps lay in wait for the mariner. Basic charting *had* been carried out by Captain James Cook in 1770, but Parry's more painstaking work in 1899 included the finding of a rock carrying just four feet of water at low tide near the Decapolis Reef and a rock carrying 24 feet of water at low tide right in the navigation 'track recommended' north of Cape Flinders.

As anywhere, the weather was the lightship crewman's principal adversary and in Queensland waters it could be spectacular. During the dry season lightning storms that cracked the heavens spilled not a single drop of rain from multi-coloured skies. In 'the wet' between December and March, rain fell with an intensity that could cause physical injury. It was also the season for cyclones and the men kept an anxious eye on the eastern horizon for tell-tale signs of any new storm gathering in the Coral Sea.

In recent years, however, such worries had begun to wane. The very worst storms, with the exception of that in March, 1893 when a number of schooners were lost off the north-east tip of the Cape York Peninsula, had occurred much further south. The pearlers were starting to look on the 1893 storm as a one-off. The owners of the boats had not bothered with insurance for years. This sense of complacency was fortified by a British Admiralty hydrographic chart of the time placing Princess Charlotte Bay 350 kilometres north of the cyclone belt.

For Fuhrman and his crew, the Saturday birthday celebrations and the proximity of the happy-go-lucky people of the fleets must have been welcome distractions from watching the reef sharks lazily circling their ship, waiting for the next bucket of slops to be dumped over the side.

The first omen of what was to come arrived in the form of flocks of storm birds and other seabirds swarming in panicky droves towards the land. Dense black clouds began to blot the eastern horizon and from within the folds of this menacing cloak forked the first flashes of lightning. No one could recall hearing any thunder. Day turned to dusk in the sudden way of the tropics and with the change came a light rain. The barometer began to fall and by 7 pm was reading 29.6 inches. The breeze stiffened sharply, swung from south-south-east to south-west and quickly increased in strength. By 10 pm the glass read 29.1 inches. What now fell upon the jumble of boats and the *Channel Rock* Lightship was to prove the worst natural disaster in the history of Queensland.

As the barometer went into freefall, above the heads of the doomed fleet cyclones Mahina and Nachon collided, wrenching the sea into a confused turmoil. Beautiful Bathurst Bay became a hell on earth as lightning seared the sky and rain thundered down. Dozens of the smaller vessels were rolled over and over, many snapping their masts on the bottom of the bay.

The schooner *Silvery Wave* was fighting a losing battle for survival. In desperation her skipper, Captain Jefferson, let go his ship's anchors. Surely he could not have known there was less than three fathoms of water under his keel. Now tethered like a goat to a stake, the *Silvery Wave* was pounded time after time into the seabed. Ill in a bunk below decks, a Japanese crewman named Sugimoto was thrown clear into the sea and somehow managed to reach the shore alive.

As though dissatisfied with dismantling Jefferson's ship, the storm also contrived to dash her disintegrating hull against the 84-ton schooner *Sagitta*. A few shattered planks were eventually recovered from the *Silvery Wave*. Of the *Sagitta* no trace was found until a lone lifebelt was washed up on a beach 160 kilometres further south. The night was so black that some crews took to firing rifles – kept aboard as a defence for divers against sharks – to alert other boats as to their position, hoping to avoid collision.

One ship which managed to ride out the storm was the 112-ton *Crest of the Wave* which had been at anchor in the lee of Cape Melville. The skipper, Captain W. Field Porter, whose wife and 18-month-old daughter were on board, said three schooners, the two already destroyed and the 25-ton tender *Admiral* which also sunk, had been anchored nearby with about 40 luggers closer inshore. The *Crest of the Wave* began to drag her anchor. A second anchor failed to halt the ship.

'Enormous waves broke over us time and time again,' said Captain Porter.

His stern dinghy and port whaleboat were carried away and the bulwarks vanished overboard. By 4.30 am Porter spoke of a lull lasting about ten minutes. The storm was taking a breather. Now it altered its angle of attack and rounded on the battered remnants of the fleet from the north-west with a venom that threw the *Crest of the Wave* on her beam ends and almost buried her in huge seas.

Shortly thereafter the entire bay was engulfed by an ocean surge – a tidal wave 13 to 15 metres high. As it struck Captain Porter's ship, cabin windows were smashed and compartments began to fill with water. But here, when all seemed lost, the extraordinary resilience of the human spirit showed itself in all its glory. Working in impossible conditions with the vessel on its side and partly submerged, Porter, a six foot, raw-boned New Zealander, somehow managed to get on deck and cut away the masts with an axe. Painfully the *Crest of the Wave* staggered back to an upright position, her starboard whaleboat now gone.

Below decks, Mrs Porter was fighting for the survival of herself and her daughter. She stood guard over the child's bunk until the rising water forced her into action. She picked up the little girl and staggered through a half-submerged companionway to another cabin, only for its windows to burst open. The weight of the inrushing ocean knocked her off her feet and the girl was gone.

'I groped for her in the dark until I found her, gasping for air,' said Mrs Porter. *'I could not keep my feet and was in the act of falling again when my husband came and steadied us and guided us through to the dining cabin where we remained clinging to whatever would help us. My husband told us we were sinking fast but when daylight came we were still afloat. When the leaks had been repaired and the water baled out, we were out of danger.'*

By 10 am the worst of the storm had passed. Porter and his crew, working frantically all night baling and stuffing anything they could lay their hands on into the holes in their ship, had won through. Of all the craft in Bathurst Bay, only the broken and battered *Crest of the Wave* was still afloat. She had been driven 24 kilometres from her original anchorage. In the space of ten hours 307 seamen and family members had died and more than 50 vessels had been destroyed.

The *Channel Rock* Lightship had vanished. It was two days before its disappearance began to cause anxiety elsewhere. First word that she was missing came from the captain of the British India steamer *Duke of Norfolk*, who was later criticised for not stopping to look for survivors despite steaming through waters choked with clues as to what had occurred. His excuse – there had been no distress signals to which he could respond. He wired Captain Almond, the Portmaster at Cooktown. He in turn wired Mr Forbes the Harbourmaster at Cairns and from there the steamer *Victory* was assigned to investigate.

The *Victory* took on stores for three weeks and set out to see what she could find. Only when she was off Cooktown was the full scale of the disaster realised. She steered for the scene in poor weather. Part of her brief was now to dispose of bodies.

On March 9th at 4.45 pm she sighted the body of a man 'torn under the arms, down the face and legs' – mutilations thought to be caused by sharks. An effort to sink it failed. There was no word of the method used. During the next hour 13 more bodies in the same shocking condition were spotted in the water.

Captain King of the *Victory* took his ship into Bathurst Bay and was met by an incredible sight. A forest of mastheads sprouted from the water and the remains of many vessels could be seen lying on the seabed. Of the lightship there was no sign.

At 3 pm on March 10th, Captain King received a visit from Captain Porter who asked him to find a secure anchorage for the *Crest of the Wave*. King took her in tow to Flinders Island. On the 11th, King landed six men on Pipon Island to hunt for signs of the lightship. They drew a blank. It would be March 15th before the *Brisbane Courier* reported the sighting of a piece of wreckage from the lightship, spotted on West Pipon Island by a crewman from the 92-ton schooner *Olive*, herself badly damaged in Princess Charlotte Bay.

The body of Gustav Oscar Fuhrman was eventually recovered and buried on the mainland nearby. The doubts about the condition of Fuhrman's ship conjure up a nightmare vision to haunt the mind. Might not the vessel have gradually come apart before the fury of the elements and created a scene, illuminated by flashes of lightning, to mock the despairing eyes of a crew who had time aplenty to understand exactly what it meant?

What happened on the land during the storm was recounted by a Constable J.M. Kenny from the Eight Mile police station near Cooktown.

His report read:

I reached Barron Point on March 3rd and camped with four native troopers on a ridge 40 feet above sea level, half a mile from the beach with scrub and a high sandy ridge between camp and beach. About 11.30 pm on the 5th, it began to blow very stiff from the south-east. At midnight the troopers' tent carried away and they came into mine. Ten minutes later this was demolished by a tree limb. Lucky to be alive, all hands made for the biggest open space near, guided by vivid lightning. It was necessary to cover the face and hands with blankets to keep off the rain which was hitting as hard as hail. About 2 am the wind veered a couple of points and blew with hurricane force. At 5 am it shifted to the north-east and blew harder than ever.

Shortly afterwards an enormous tidal wave swept inshore and reached waist-deep on the ridge with the camp on it. It was not proper daylight until about 10 am on the Sunday. On mustering horses, we found four had been killed by trees.

Whole areas of scrub were blown flat, trees uprooted and all those left standing stripped of bark and leaves. We found the deepest encroachment of the tidal wave to be six kilometres inland. The wind reached 200 kilometres per hour. Huge tracts of mangroves along the coast vanished.

In some of the trees which remained upright near the coastline, wind-driven stones were found embedded to a depth of 15 centimetres. The stench of death was everywhere. As well as human corpses, thousands of dead porpoises, dolphins, fish and reptiles and even sharks were heaped in grotesque confusion an hour's walk from the water's edge. Constable Kenny's party buried 37 bodies. A few had to be fetched down from trees which offered the unpleasant complication of serving as a temporary refuge for some of the most dangerous snakes on the planet. In the steaming heat of the Queensland summer in air thick with insects, it is hard to imagine a more odious task.

Where there was death aplenty however, life produced its own remarkable examples of tenacious survival. People were rescued after five days in the water, having swum from reef to reef, subsisting on any marine life they could find. A Japanese diver by the name of Seto had to fight the storm on his own aboard the lugger *Estelle*. Although he had no sail hoisted, the mast was snapped like a twig. He anchored the ship but she was pushed around like a toy in a bath. All night Seto tried to keep the vessel's head to wind. He too experienced the same lull as Captain Porter and used the precious few minutes to begin pumping out the ship. To no avail. As the storm struck again the *Estelle* was overwhelmed. Seto clung for hours to the wreckage and was eventually picked up.

Most heartbreaking of all the tales to emerge from the other side of the maelstrom was that of two young native wives and their two children. Pitched into the sea when their small boat was swamped they made for land with the youngsters clinging on to their long flowing hair. It was daybreak before the women staggered ashore on an island. The children were still with them, tiny fists locked in their mothers' tresses – but alas, no longer alive.

Grizzled old ships' captains and aged Aborigines could recall nothing like the clash of the cyclones in the scope of their memory. Little wonder. During the storm a barometric pressure reading of 20 inches was observed, the lowest ever in Australia.

Today, a white memorial stone that is hard to find among the scrub and rocks at Bathurst Bay, recalls the cyclones in terms which speak volumes for the attitudes of the day. Nine of the 12 white people lost are named, including the lightship crewmen and Mr Alfred Outridge, whose grave the stone marks, but the others are classed simply as 'over 300 coloured men'. It isn't even accurate – included among the dead were scores of women and children. Neither does it take account of those Aborigines who met their deaths all along the shoreline. They had acted with the greatest courage and humanity, looking after survivors at the height of the storm and helping to bury the dead. Many had been so engaged when the tidal wave struck, sweeping them away like so many leaves.

Their contribution was marked with gifts of tobacco, pipes, shirts, dresses, tomahawks, knives and flour, distributed by the Harbourmaster at Cooktown and a Dr Roth who had organised a special expedition north in a cutter to deliver the goods.

A return compiled later in the year by George H. Bennett, Inspector of Pearl-Shell and Bêche-de-Mer Fisheries made sobering reading. It showed the loss of vessels as follows: Schooners–3; Tenders to Schooners–1; Diving Boats–35; Swimming Boats–12; Tortoiseshell Boats–2; Bêche-de-Mer Boats–1. A total of 54 craft.

A proclamation issued shortly after the disaster banned pearl-shell fishing between latitudes 11 degrees, 58 minutes, 30 seconds south, and Cape Grafton in latitude 16 degrees, 52 minutes. The prohibition lasted from January 1st until April 15th in the years 1900, 1901 and 1902.

But the undersea riches of the Queensland coast proved too powerful a lure to allow the perils of acquiring them to blunt that challenge. Less than one year after the disaster, the pearl-shell fleet was not just back to full strength, it was bigger than ever. In a report on the situation in January, 1900 Bennett noted this with satisfaction from his base on Thursday Island.

However, it is interesting to discover a tone of some regret in terms of the efficiency of the new fleet. The report stated:

> *The shortage of labour caused has never entirely been made good. Many of the men lost were trained and experienced divers and tenders and some time must elapse before their places can be satisfactorily filled.*

Pearling fleets were periodically decimated by cyclones. The boats working in Exmouth Gulf, Western Australia were swamped on Christmas Eve, 1875 with the loss of 59 lives. Eighteen months later another fleet lost 22 vessels and 140 men at 90-mile Beach (now known as 80-mile Beach), Western Australia, and on March 13th, 1934, an intense cyclone in northern Queensland destroyed many pearling boats and killed 30 crewmen.

Of all violent weather systems, tropical cyclones carry the heaviest punch. In the southern hemisphere they circulate clockwise opposed to the counter-clockwise movement of winds in northern hemisphere storms. They appeared to favour the festive season to raise their fists against Australian doors. On Christmas Eve and Christmas Day, 1971, cyclone Althea wrecked much of Townsville and on Christmas Day three years later much of the Northern Territory capital city of Darwin was flattened by cyclone Tracy which achieved wind speeds of 217 kilometres per hour.

In the immediate aftermath of the 1899 disaster, a relief lightship was brought from Cooktown and placed near the Channel Rock but closer to Pipon Island. The reason was a clear reluctance to place the crew at the same risk as their dead colleagues and a land-based system was evolved to run the lightship. The crew lived on the stone-strewn island and serviced the ship by boat. To get there they pulled themselves hand over hand by cable, a method not unlike that used in the United States to service small river lightboats in the early 19th century. This was a temporary arrangement, lasting about 18 months, for the fate of the lightship station was sealed. The *Channel Rock* had always been a difficult site, the anchor often dragging in rough weather. Just six weeks after the cyclone, the relief lightship was blown five kilometres out of position.

In 1901, a new fixed light shown from an iron tower 65 feet above sea level was placed on West Pipon Island. It bore a fourth order dioptric light, intensified in the direction of the most intricate section of the channel and it displayed an arc of red light extending to 23 degrees over the Channel Rock in a type of coloured sectoring that was quite common in those times. The light was visible at a distance of 22 kilometres, well in excess of the lightship's beam.

Although the case for the removal of the lightship was compelling, the increased range of the land-based light flattered to deceive. There can be little doubt that the traffic using the narrow channel sorely missed the ship in daylight and in thick weather the absence of her fog signal close to the rock must have spawned the deepest anxiety.

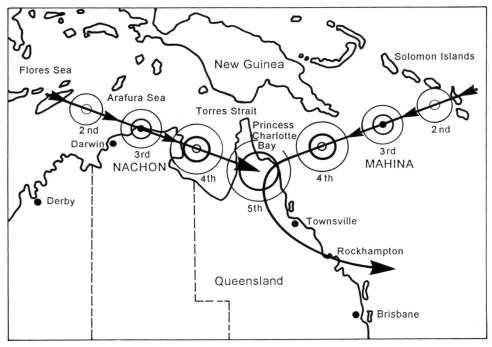

The clash of the titans. Cyclones Mahina and Nachon combined forces to bring about Queensland's worst natural disaster.

Deeper still into the vast emptiness of the western Pacific lies the Merkara Shoal, at 160 kilometres from Thursday Island, beyond the practical scope of a manned light vessel. This hazard became the first in Australian waters to be marked by an unmanned lightship, built at the Cockatoo Dockyard in Sydney in 1916/17, one of four such vessels.

Two were named *Carpentaria* and alternated at the Merkara Shoal, the other two bore the name *Breaksea Spit*, marking Sandy Cape at the southern edge of the great Barrier Reef. With one lightship on duty, the other was held in reserve. Occasionally the ships would be used at other locations. Each of these light vessels was 70 feet long, weighed 164 tonnes and carried a bell worked by the motion of the ships. The light was fuelled by acetylene gas of which a six-month supply was carried in tanks.

Designers D & C Stevenson of Edinburgh provided the plans for the ships based on their *Otter Rock* Lightship prototype. This vessel was first anchored in 16

Commonwealth Lightship No. 4, a fully automated vessel, bears the name *Carpentaria* in recognition of its long asociation with the Merkara Shoal station at the western entrance to the Gulf of Carpentaria. The ship, scarcely altered since it was built more than 80 years ago, is in the collection of the Australian National Maritime Museum at Darling Harbour, Sydney.
Photograph by Jenni Carter is reproduced courtesy of the ANMM.

fathoms off Port Ellen on the south-east coast of the island of Islay in 1901. However, the spectacularly increased effectiveness of these ships hinged upon a Swedish invention.

Nobel Prize-winning physicist Nils Gustav Dalen had created the automatic Sunvalve or Solventil in 1912. This ingenious contraption consisted of a fat metal tube coated in lampblack – a kind of liquidised carbon – ringed by three slim, polished rods. Dalen was taking advantage of the fact that the dulled surface absorbed radiated light even on cloudy days, and warmed up and expanded while the polished rods reflected the light and remained unaffected by it. A pin extending from the base of the expanding tube pressed onto a sensitive valve which regulated the flow of acetylene gas to the light, turning it off. As daylight faded, the dulled tube cooled and contracted and the pin rose off the valve, so allowing the free passage of gas which was ignited by a pilot light burning 24 hours a day. The Sunvalve was able to permit the movement of all the lengths of metal as the result of heat or cold since they expanded and contracted at the same rate. Only daylight, or the disappearance of it, made enough difference to activate the valve. Dalen's invention was encased in glass, looking for all the world like a tiny lantern. By ensuring the light operated just at night, the Sunvalve effectively doubled the time a light could remain unattended while using the same amount of fuel.

Much initial scepticism greeted the Sunvalve. It had been dismissed as 'unworkable' by no less an authority than Thomas Edison, inventor among many other things of the incandescent electric light bulb. Even with the Sunvalve in successful operation, Edison's stubborn streak overcame common sense and he refused to acknowledge Dalen's triumph. While Edison had to spend much of his life profoundly deaf, Dalen had to spend much of his minus his sight. In 1913 he was blinded in a quarry accident while carrying out an experiment but was able to continue with his innovative work until his death from cancer in 1937.

A most rare and fascinating insight into the lightship life of Australia is offered by a yachtsman passing the *Piper Island* Lightship. The text of his observations is contained in a publication of 1889 entitled *Cassell's Picturesque Australasia*, edited by E.E. Morris and recreated today in pages from Australia's First Century 1788–1888.

The yachtsman's view may be flawed in part but his 'feel' for the subject tellingly imparts the sense of solitude endured by those who kept the light burning so that people whom they could not see, did not know nor would ever meet, might pass safely through the night.

He writes:

We pass a lightship and on the poop a woman waves either her dishtowel or dirty handkerchief at us. We respond, wondering how this hermit life and awful ocean monotony suits her, and how she still retains vivacity enough even to signal passing vessels, with that everlasting sound of lapping waters about her contracted prison and that nearly everlasting sunshine and smooth water. Does she agree all the better with her husband now that she is shut in day after day and week after week with him and his mate, with the sky blazing hot and the deck like an oven, with the unvaried round of sardines, sheeps' tongues and tinned salt meat and only a rare storm to give change to her uneventful life?

Will washing the decks and dishes be the same as washing the floors and dishes ashore? I think if I were a light-keeper I should grow tired of the golden sunrises and orange sunsets, of the silver moonlights and cloudless, star-lit nights. The sight of those heavy, tropical, electric-charged clouds forking out their random flashes would be a glad relief, the rattle of Heaven's musketry sweet music.

The lightship is painted red and pointed with white, is one-masted and has a railed-in lookout. The sun may blister its paintwork, or the sudden furious gales make it groan and labour at its chains but there is no danger, as there is no motion.

The decks look clean and, with the woman on board there are articles lying about which give it a little of the appearance of land. Land however, is far distant and land such as they see is held by cruel, senseless savages.

Now and again a steamer passes the lightship, giving to its inmates a hasty glimpse of other humanity and even so doing something, though it be but little, to relieve the monotony of their existence.

Occasionally a vessel will stop to supply them with fresh provisions but having transferred these to the small boat belonging to the lightship, it loses no time in once more getting under way.

By day, as the lightship basks in the sun, it is a welcome sight to passing vessels, a milestone on the way; and at night, with the great stars shining above it, and its near golden light blazing out and rippling down the broken waters, it is a cheering and heart-warming spectacle; but to those on board, who night after night only see the dusky-looking halo round the lamp-disc, who day after day go up to trim it, what must it become? They give light and life and variety to others, burning their own hearts away with the weariness of monotonous, dreary duty.

The fact of a woman being on board is an eye-opener and may be a measure of the difficulty in securing crews for the lightships in those times and in those places. Or it may reflect the stark choice facing a married couple in that service. Does the man vanish for years on end alone, or does he take his spouse with him? In either case their employers were hardly in a position to complain. On later lightships in Denmark, stewardesses were sometimes employed.

The *Piper Island* and *Claremont Island* lightships were decommissioned about 1918.

The Falls Lightship

*I*t seemed like a good idea at the time. Members of the Belgian watersports club *Les Pneumatiques* hit upon the adventurous notion of taking a fleet of their powered rubber dinghies on a shopping expedition to England. From their base at the port of Antwerp on the River Scheldt, members, friends and their families – a party of 60 all told – headed for Dunkirk from which point they would tackle the English Channel crossing to the Kent town of Ramsgate 35 miles away.

It was late May, 1977. The weather in the Channel was fine and the shoppers were in high spirits as their powerful engines propelled them towards the chalky shores of England. Lightships were observed, both French and English. These included the *Falls* Lightship anchored 10 miles off Broadstairs.

The group arrived in Ramsgate on Friday the 27th. Their weekend spending spree had the shopkeepers of Ramsgate and Dover rubbing their hands at this un-expected bonus from the continent before the flotilla prepared to embark on the return trip from Ramsgate, laden with parcels worth about £3000. It was Sunday afternoon. Suddenly, things began to go wrong.

As the boats emerged from the lee of the land, they were assailed by force 6/7 winds from the north-east. The waves became higher and higher as the shore receded further behind them. It grew bitterly cold. The dinghies were beginning to ship a lot of water and the initial mood of tired contentment was replaced in short order by one of deep anxiety. Safety was now the paramount concern.

The group leader, Dr Vladimir Kozireff, decided they should abandon any notion of trying for Dunkirk and head instead for the *Falls* Lightship. As the weather continued to worsen, the battle to reach the *Falls* became a freezing, soaking night-mare, and finally ended when all 24 inflatables got alongside. It had taken the group 4½ hours to travel just 14 miles. Willing hands heaved aboard the entire group of 60, including three children. Many were suffering from exposure and seasickness.

Master of the lightship, William Semple, advised the Ramsgate lifeboat of his peculiar situation and that vessel launched, as did the Margate lifeboat, and headed

The *Falls* Lightship. Photograph Fotoflite, Ashford, Kent.

for the *Falls*. It was 6.45 pm. On board the lightship the unexpected guests were busy making link calls home. The initial feeling was one of relief. All were safe and no-one was missing.

However, in the first of several alarms which would characterise the incident, the M.V. *Barok* reported a dinghy drifting 3½ miles south of the *Falls* with no-one on board. A rescue helicopter from RAF Manston was about to take off when it was confirmed that the dinghy had broken free from the group tied up to the lightship. The helicopter stood down.

En route to the *Falls*, Ramsgate lifeboat coxswain Ron Cannon contacted the skipper of the cross-channel ferry *Olau West*, on its way to Dunkirk, and asked if he would stop at the lightship and take off the Belgians. He did stop, only to discover that just two people were prepared to join his ship. The skipper was not amused.

When Cannon and his crew arrived, another 18 reluctantly boarded the lifeboat for the return trip to Ramsgate. On the way back Cannon had to arange for an ambulance to meet them at the quayside where two of the party were removed to hospital for treatment for hypothermia and extreme seasickness. The Margate boat, which had provided back-up throughout the operation, also returned to base. It was now 10.21 pm.

William Semple still had 40 distressed and increasingly irritated passengers aboard his ship. He reported:

'You can imagine what it is like. There are bodies spread everywhere, sleeping in the decks and the galley and wherever else they can get their heads down. We have one child on board, a boy of 11, and his mother. We are cooking meals with anything we can lay our hands on. Some are so seasick they don't feel like eating. They are not very pleased with the British weather forecasters.'

In Ramsgate, some of the Belgians were now expressing concern over four to six of their number who had decided to leave the lightship about 7 pm, bound for Dunkirk. They could not be traced and early on the 30th a broadcast to all shipping in the area was initiated. Confusion reigned as two dinghies were reported entering Ramsgate harbour, possibly from the lightship. The *Falls* confirmed that two boats *had* left for Ramsgate but added the further unwelcome information that yet another had set out on its own for Dunkirk.

At 8 am a Belgian helicopter took off from Ostend to search the area between the *Falls* and Dunkirk. Reports were now coming in thick and fast of other dinghies adrift, nine having become separated from the lightship during a night of continued heavy weather. A message was received advising that the two dinghies which had left the *Falls* at 7 the previous evening were now safely in Dunkirk harbour. Just one manned boat remained to be traced.

About noon on the 30th the Trinity House vessel *Ready* evacuated the main group from the lightship and headed for Dover. During the short trip there the rescue centre at Ostend reported the final dinghy had been accounted for. According to the Belgian news agency Belga its occupant, M. Pol Andre, of Brussels, had arrived home tired out after a gruelling cross-channel voyage and gone straight to bed. In the morning he heard on the radio that one of his group was still missing. Full of concern he called the Ostend centre for information, only to discover that the missing person was none other than himself.

At Dover, 35 deflated *Pneumatiques* were met by the Belgian Consul who arranged for them to be sent home on the first available ferry. A Trinity House spokesman said: 'This club outing was totally irresponsible. The people arrived wet and angry and it will be a long time before they do this sort of thing again.' There was understandable frustration in this remark but it is undeniable that the forecast for the area was misleading. The forecast published in *The Times* on Saturday 28th for the east Channel from 6 am until midnight Sunday read: *Wind north-east moderate or fresh. Sea slight or moderate.*

What the party got was a near-storm, the sea conditions logged in the Ramsgate lifeboat's report as 'rough'. Dr Kozireff hotly denied his group had been irresponsible. He said: *'I have watched TV interviews with people, among them Coastguard officers, and much of what they had to say has been plain fantasy.'* Dr Kozireff claimed he had again checked the weather at Ramsgate before leaving. He went on: *'There was no panic or distress. But there were people who were very tired and that and the weather conditions, and a mechanical problem, made me decide to abandon.'*

However another group member, 38-year old company director Claude Remy, made the point that no such trips should be made again with women and children.

'I think it is too dangerous for them,' he said. *'They are all exhausted.'*

The Belgians were not the only ones caught out by the sudden change in the weather. Nine ambulancemen from Sheffield had left on a charity enterprise from Boulogne early on Sunday in perfect weather. They had set themselves to row across the Channel in a whaler belonging to the Royal Marines. Five miles off Dover they were caught in the same gale as *Les Pneumatiques* and found themselves being swept westwards along the English coast. They sent out a distress call on a hand-held radio. A fishing boat stood by them and a light aircraft patrolled overhead until, on a busy day for lifeboats, the Dover boat reached them. For all concerned it could have been so much worse.

If the Belgian bargain-hunters cared to reflect today on their ill-fated trip, they might do well to consider a question that must surely dispatch a shiver down the full length of their spines: What if we'd made the trip nine or ten years later?

In 1986 the *Falls* light vessel station went automatic. From that year on, as a haven of comfort and security it became useless. As a point from which a rescue could be effected or co-ordinated it embraced immediate compulsory redundancy. And what in 1977 turned out to be a great inconvenience for shoppers, lifeboatmen, a lightship crew, helicopter pilots, Coastguards, etc would have ended up in 1987 as – what?

Footnote: The automatic ship was itself replaced on March 4th, 1993 by a lighted buoy.

LV *Pharos*

Of life aboard the first lightships few accurate accounts remain, although some fair assumptions can be made. That it was uncomfortable in the extreme is certain. Also, the hazards of the job were compounded in those far-off times by unsound ships, poor moorings and the fact that the vessels used were crude, hasty conversions from colliers, traders or ships captured in wartime.

It is a matter of record that the world's first-ever lightship, positioned close to the Nore buoy at the confluence of the rivers Thames and Medway in 1732, was blown ashore several times to the great alarm of the crew yet quickly earned the affection of the seamen plying these congested waters. To steer them past the Nore sandbank at night the lightship carried two lanterns 12 feet apart on a cross beam fixed to the mast. The lanterns appeared to be secured at right angles to the yard and not permitted to swing freely. Tallow candles inside forced a dull yellow glow a bare few hundred yards beyond the ship.

Scotland's first lightship boasted three lanterns, first set aglow ten miles off Arbroath in the late summer of 1807. They were destined to cast fresh illumination upon the entire world of coastal navigation. For the man who designed them was legendary Scots engineer Robert Stevenson, about to begin construction of one of his 'impossible' projects, the Bell Rock lighthouse. His converted lightship was anything but crude. This product of a mind that was a potent mix of precision and imagination was the most advanced lightship then afloat.

The ship, the *Pharos*, was in fact a multi-purpose vessel. In addition to acting as a seamark north-west of the Bell Rock while the tower was being built there, she provided accommodation for the lighthouse artificers and for Stevenson, whose cabin contained a small library, as well as for the crew, officers and the principal lightkeeper. All 48 people were crammed into 67 feet, the overall length of the *Pharos* and squeezed in a lateral direction as well, the breadth of the ship on deck being a mere 16 feet.

As a considerable compensation for this, rations were good by the standards of the day with copious quantities of beef, biscuit, oatmeal, barley, butter, beer, rum, vegetables and salt being kept on board. Space also had to be found for the necessities of the ship – sperm whale oil, wicks, ropes, oars, spare sails, etc.

By Act of Parliament, the Commissioners of Northern Lights were empowered to levy light dues on British vessels sailing to, from or within a line drawn from Berwick to Peterhead of one penny halfpenny per register ton of cargo carried and threepence on foreign ships, thus cannily defraying the capital costs involved in building the lighthouse.

The *Pharos* had a troubled start to her career as a lightship. When the crew mustered at Leith to take her out for the first time, Stevenson was in the process of greeting them when, as the engineer later wrote:

Two of the seamen having taken alarm at the destination of the ship and the nature of the service in which they were about to embark, turned about and, to the great surprise of their companions, ran with the utmost precipitation from the ship, to which they never again returned.

The terrified twosome were replaced without delay and the ship set sail at 8 am on July 10th with a crew of 12 under Captain George Sinclair. Also on board was veteran Yarmouth pilot Joseph Webb, whose services Stevenson had acquired on the advice of Trinity House, London. Webb had had a major success in fitting up a floating light off the Norfolk coast.

From the start the *Pharos* proved a cumbersome vessel to handle and made hard work of getting downriver as far as the Isle of May where she anchored at 6 pm. The lighthouse yacht carrying the floating light's main moorings had easily caught up with her and anchored nearby rather than risk approaching the Bell Rock after dark. Observed from the yacht that evening, the *Pharos* appeared to roll so much 'that she was in some danger of making a round turn and appearing with her keel uppermost'. This behaviour was the source of some amusement although the violent antics of the ship were to become legendary in the lighthouse service and were not regarded with a like degree of hilarity by those living and working aboard.

Next day saw near disaster. The yacht lost overboard every particle of the floating light's moorings, which vanished with a roar and a rush into 17 fathoms of water. Many anxious hours were spent fishing for them and they were finally hooked by a grappling iron a short way from the anchor itself.

What had then to take place was an operation fraught with danger and difficulty as every available piece of tackle from the yacht and the *Pharos* were employed to raise a weight estimated at three tons from the seabed. At any time the tenuous hold on the anchor chain could have been lost, causing mayhem among the working teams above. It took 14 hours of back-breaking work by the full crews of both vessels, 'neither hand-spike nor tackle five minutes out of their hands' during this time, to get the moorings back on board. Refreshments were served as the men slaved at the purchases and at the windlass of the floating light.

The best spot for the *Pharos* to put down her permanent mooring was a matter of great concern and the ship was only set in place after consultations with 'nautical gentlemen' from Arbroath and with a committee which had been formed among the captains of Trinity House, Leith.

The lighthouse workers were not introduced to their floating barrack for some weeks but on their first Saturday night afloat, August 23rd, an impromptu party took place. All hands were served with a glass of rum and water to drink the sailor's favourite toast – wives and sweethearts. The ship's company assembled in the galley and musical instruments were produced. Every man had to play a tune, sing a song or tell a story amid much boisterous mirth which apparently increased as the night went on and access to the on-board supplies of good small beer remained uninterrupted. The men, according to the lighthouse engineer, 'appeared to suffer from no want whatsoever'.

Stevenson's accomplishments are well documented but little attention has been paid to the risks run by this hands-on genius in pursuit of his craft. He was indeed lucky to have had the chance to tackle the Bell Rock at all. In 1794, in the course of a voyage to Edinburgh from Orkney on the sloop *Elizabeth*, Stevenson asked to be put on the beach when the wind dropped to nothing and the vessel was becalmed off Kinnaird Head, Fraserburgh. He was rowed ashore and continued his journey overland. Within hours a southerly gale sprang up and the *Elizabeth* was driven all the way back to Orkney where she was wrecked with the loss of all hands.

But Stevenson did not miss the first storm endured by the *Pharos* and her complement. His account of the ordeal serves as a reminder of the perils of the profession and as a rare, classic illustration of life in heavy seas aboard an early lightship. The date is Sunday, September 6th, 1807, nine days before the light of the *Pharos* was due to be lit for the first time. He writes:

> *During the last night there was little rest on board as the gale continued with unabated violence.*
>
> *The sea struck so hard upon the bows that it rose in great quantities or in 'green seas' as the sailors termed it, which were carried by the wind as far aft as the quarter deck and not infrequently over the stern altogether. It fell so heavily on the skylight of the writer's cabin that the glass was broken to pieces before the deadlight could be got into place so that water poured in in great quantities. In shutting out the water the admission of light was prevented and all morning continued in the most comfortless state of darkness.*
>
> *About 10 am the wind shifted to north-east and blew, if possible, harder than before. In this state things remained during the whole day. Every sea which struck the vessel – and the seas followed each other in close succession – caused her to shake and all on board occasionally to tremble. At times her motion was felt as if she had either broken adrift or was in the act of sinking. At about 11 am the writer, with some difficulty, got out of bed but in attempting to dress was thrown twice upon the floor at the opposite side of the cabin.*
>
> *In an undressed state he made shift to get about halfway up the companion stairs to observe the state of the sea and of the ship on deck but he no sooner looked over the companion than a heavy sea struck, fell on the quarter deck and*

rushed downstairs into the cabin in so considerable a quantity that it was found necessary to lift one of the scuttles in the floor to let the water into the limbers of the ship as it dashed from side to side in such a manner as to run into the lower tier of beds. Being completely wetted, the writer got below and went to bed.

In this state of weather the seamen had to move about the necessary duties of the ship with the most cautious use of hands and feet while it required all the art of the landsman to keep himself within the precincts of his bed. The writer found himself so much tossed about that it became necessary in some measure to shut himself in bed in order to avoid being thrown upon the floor.

About 2 pm a great alarm was given throughout the ship from the effects of a very heavy sea which almost filled the waist, pouring down into the berths below through every chink and crevice of the hatches and skylights. From the motion of the vessel being thus suddenly deadened or checked and from the flowing in of water from above, it is believed there was not an individual on board who did not think at that moment that the vessel was in the act of sinking.

The writer could withstand this no longer and as soon as she began again to range to the sea, he determined to make another effort to get upon deck.

In the first instance he groped his way in darkness from his own cabin through the berths of the officers where all was quietness. He next entered the galley and other compartments occupied by the artificers: here also was shut in darkness, the fire having been drowned out in the early part of the gale: several artificers were employed in prayer, repeating psalms and other devotional exercises in full tone of voice: others protesting that if they should fortunately get once more upon the shore, no one should ever see them afloat again. With assistance from the landing master the writer made his way, holding on step by step among the numerous impediments which lay in the way.

Such was the creaking of the bulkheads, the dashing of the water and whistling of the wind that it was hardly possible to break in upon such a confusion of sounds.

The next berth was that allotted to the seamen. Here the scene was considerably different.

Having reached the middle of this darksome berth, without its inmates being aware of any intrusion, the writer had the consolation of remarking that although they talked of bad weather and the cross accidents of the sea, yet the conversation was carried out in that sort of tone or manner which bespoke an ease and composure of mind.

It being impossible to open any of the hatches in that fore part of the ship, the watch was changed by passing through the several berths to the companion stair leading to the quarter deck. The writer therefore made the best of his way aft again and on a second attempt to look out, saw an astonishing sight. The waves appeared to be ten or fifteen feet in height of unbroken water and each approaching billow seemed as if it would overwhelm our vessel but she continued to rise upon the waves and to fall between the seas in a very wonderful manner.

On deck there was one solitary individual looking out to give the alarm in the event of the ship breaking from her moorings.

The seaman on watch continued for only two hours; he who kept watch at this time was a tall, slender man of black complexion; he had no greatcoat nor overall of any kind but was simply dressed in his ordinary jacket and trousers; his hat was tied under his chin with a napkin and he stood aft the foremast to which he had lashed himself with a gasket or small rope round his waist to prevent himself falling on deck or being washed overboard. When the writer looked up he appeared to smile. This person was as wetted as if he had been drawn through the sea, which was given as the reason for his not putting on his greatcoat, that he might wet few clothes and have a dry shift when he went below.

By this time – about 3 pm – the gale had continued unabated for 27 hours. The writer thought it necessary to advise the master and officers as to the probable event of the vessel's drifting from her moorings. They gave it as their opinion that we now had every chance of riding out the gale and that even if she should part from her anchor, the storm sails had been laid to hand and could be bent in a very short time.

At about 6 pm the ship's company were heard moving about on deck and the writer rang his bell to know what was the matter. He was informed that the weather looked better and that the men were trying to rig the smoke funnel of the galley so that cooking could commence. The writer himself had had nothing to eat for 21 hours. The cook lit the galley fire and set to make suet pudding. By 9 pm all hands had been refreshed by the exertions of the cook and the steward. The usual complement of men was now also set on watch and more quietness experienced throughout the ship although she was now pitching heavily instead of rolling.

Although the previous night had been a very restless one, it had not the effect of inducing repose in the writer's berth on the succeeding night for having been so much tossed about in bed during the last thirty hours, he found no easy spot to turn to and his body was all sore to the touch, which ill accorded with the unyielding materials with which his bed-place was surrounded.

Next day, although the sea was still running high – Stevenson estimated the height of the spray to be 40 or 50 feet – the sun shone and the business of drying out clothes and bunks began. By noon conditions were much better but it was now realised to everyone's astonishment that the ship was adrift!

The writer continued:

The mizzen and other sails were set and we bore away about one mile to the south-west of the former station and there let go the best bower anchor and cable in twenty fathoms of water to ride until the sea should fall when it might be practicable to grapple for the moorings and find a better anchorage for the ship.

The cable was hove up and was found to have parted about fifty fathoms from the chain moorings. If this accident had happened during the storm, the floating light must inevitably have gone ashore on the Bell Rock.

That part of the cable which consisted of rope had not worn through – it had been severed by some underwater obstruction, possibly part of a wreck. The *Pharos* was moved from her original anchorage 1½ miles from the rock to a new site another half a mile further north-west. She never again broke loose during her three and a half years' service although on many occasions she lived up to the observation made by one crew member that she could turn a halfpenny laid flat on the deck.

Included in the remarkable achievements associated with the lighthouse project was the loss of not a single life at sea during construction. Yet each time the workers went to the rock they had to be rowed there from the *Pharos* then rowed back in two boats, often in poor weather. It was the task of the landing master to assemble the workers for the trip to the rock. As soon as the highest point of the reef appeared above the waves a signal bell was sounded and the landing master called out: 'All hands to the rock!' The men worked in rain, snow, fog and wind, provided it did not cause the waves to break too heavily upon the rock.

A one-way trip usually took 20 minutes but could take up to three hours with rowers and those seamen assigned to bale out the boats sometimes knee-deep in water. During the entire tour of duty the ship spent in her perilous employment more than 1,000 oars were broken. This would not have happened but for an administrative error which resulted in an order for a large number of oars made of fir instead of the far stronger ash generally used for oars. After any especially difficult passage back to the lightship, the crews were given an extra tot of rum.

Despite the danger and the sheer hard grind of getting to and from the lighthouse site, the seamen and artificers occupying the boats ran frequent races. Competition was furious and sometimes hilarious, a situation which surprised and delighted Stevenson. Even the perils of transferring between the boats and the *Pharos* in dirty weather were reduced to a comic exercise by the ribald comments directed at the participants.

After two years the lighthouse workers moved to the rock itself to inhabit the barrack built there for them. The role of the *Pharos* reverted to that of a lightship pure and simple. When the lighthouse was completed in February, 1911, the *Pharos* was removed. On her way to Leith bad weather forced her to call in at Anstruther. Here such interest was shown in the ship and its unusual rig that people travelled for miles on foot, by carriage or on horseback to get a look at her. They also wondered at the great profusion of weed and shell on her hull.

Stevenson recalled that the crew gained such favour among the women of Anstruther and the neighbouring East Neuk towns that in the course of their short stay some of them managed to get married.

If the vessel had remained another week or two in port the probability is that she would not have had an unmarried man on board, he wrote.

When the *Pharos* reached Leith in early March she was stripped of her specialist equipment and never served again as a lightship. But even while taking her last few breaths as a floating light she was able to push out the frontiers of knowledge. Many of the marine growths which had so impressed her visitors at Anstruther turned out to be unknown to science.

Stevenson had resolved to take no action in selecting a vessel to convert into his floating light until he had visited the *Nore* Lightship in the Thames estuary, even though that vessel sat in relatively quiet waters. He concluded that a ship built after the fashion of the continental fishing doggers would be best suit his purpose.

And so the *Pharos* came to be converted from the Prussian fishing boat *Tonge Gerritt*, captured by a British cruiser while working off the Dogger Bank in the North Sea. She was flat in the bottom and rounded at both stem and stern. Stevenson, whose original intention to build a lightship from scratch had been frustrated by the expense of so doing, bought the boat for £250 and had her taken to a graving dock in Leith in March, 1807 where, among other major works such as a total re-rigging, she was given a second 'skin' with salt poured between the hulls to preserve the wood. Her bottom was sheathed in fir planking and the whole of the interior lining was caulked and made watertight in case the outer planks were breached in some mishap.

Cost of the whole conversion, including two extra masts, rose to £4171.5s.5½d, for which sum Stevenson could have had his purpose-built lightship after all. Total weight of the ship was a scanty 82 tons, extremely light for the first lightship ever to be anchored in deep water in the open sea.

The *Pharos* carried a lantern on each of her three masts, the centre mast being the highest at 35 feet, the others 25 feet. The operating height of the lanterns was set at about halfway up the masts so as not to make the ship top-heavy. A triangular pattern of light was produced which could be seen three leagues off – about nine nautical miles – a range unheard of in those times. Each lantern was of copper, about five feet in diameter and contained ten oil lamps in gimbals, all having silver-plated reflectors. This system with lamps in front of reflectors was known as 'catoptric', superseded in some later lightships by the 'dioptric' system which placed lamps behind a lens and an array of prisms.

Although the lamps of the *Pharos* were described only as 'agitable' it seems certain they were Argand burners, first patented in England in 1784 by Swiss engineer Aime Argand. Argand's invention represented the first basic change in lamp technology for thousands of years. It applied a principle later adapted to gas lamps. Argand's burner consisted of a cylindrical wick housed between two concentric metal tubes. The inner tube provided a passage through which air rose into the centre to support combustion on the inner surface of the cylindrical flame in addition to that on the outer surface. The later addition of a glass chimney increased the draught, permitting more complete burning of the oil and so cutting down on soot. An Argand lamp gave about ten times the light of earlier lamps the same size as well as a cleaner flame. However, its consumption of oil was greater.

Stevenson's lanterns encircled the masts in chandelier fashion so they could be seen from every point of the compass and could be raised and lowered from deck level. The crew of the floating light immediately christened this wonder 'The Moon Box.' A distinctive identification mark for the ship during daylight was a blue flag depicting a lighthouse, flown from the centre mast. During poor visibility a huge fog bell on the foredeck was tolled once a minute.

Robert Stevenson's revolutionary 'moon box' which appeared on a light vessel for the first time ever off the Bell Rock in 1807. The *Pharos* carried three of them, one on each mast, displaying a triangular pattern of light to provide an unmistakeable difference from the double lights at the entrance to the river Tay; from the double lights on the scares off the Northumberland coast; and from the single light on the Isle of May 17 miles to the south-west.

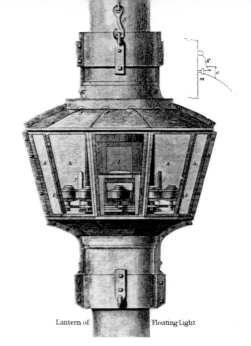

Lantern of   Floating Light

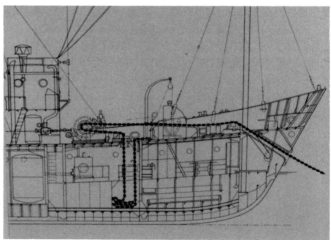

Typical arrangement of modern lightship mooring on board a vessel. The chain is drawn by the winch on deck from the chain locker below and fed out through the centre of three hawsepipes in the bow. This diagram appears on board the former British lightship *LV 4*, now part of the maritime heritage centre at Douarnenez, Brittany. Photograph courtesy of E. Koch, Hamburg.

The mooring consisted of a Stevenson-designed 1½-ton cast iron mushroom-shaped anchor which was to become standard equipment for light vessels. Its advantage over traditional anchors was beautifully simple. As the ship above tugged upon it, the lip of the mushroom bit into the seabed, gaining grip and at the same time it scooped material into the cup of the mushroom, greatly raising its weight. For the ground tackle, a 50-fathom length of 1½-inch thick chain was used (chain would not be widely used until the 1820s) and a rope 14 inches in circumference, later changed to one of 16 inches, for the main cable. These ropes when new proved stiff and unpliable and the seamen hated having to handle them.

It is no exaggeration to say that the *Pharos* was packed with new technology. Stevenson's innovations helped to lead the world into an era of floating lights which until then had been confined to European waters.

Sperm whale oil, the most prized of all the whale oils, was the only fuel used in British lightship lamps until 1846. It could be extracted from the blubber of the whale by means of try works (a boiling or melting plant) on board the whaling ships and from other small reservoirs in various parts of the 50–60 foot bodies of the adult whales. It could then be burned, once strained, in lamps. Products from the enormous square-shaped head of the animal included oil and spermaceti, a smooth white substance which was ladled out of the skull cavity in buckets. It was pressed into barrels where it solidified into a substance known as whale tallow. This was convertible into candles, cosmetics or ointments. Whale oil was not technically an oil at all but a viscous wax. A single large male sperm whale might yield three tons (80 barrels) of it.

Whalebone was another valuable product. Light and strong, it was used for stiffening bodices and corsets. The trips made by Scottish whalers to the Arctic during summer could be highly lucrative. A record cargo of the Scottish whaling fleet was achieved by the *Revolution* of Peterhead in 1814. The ship returned to port with the products of 44 whales on board. 299 tons of whale oil, spermaceti and whalebone raised £9568. Once the government bounty offered for Greenland whales in those days was added, the total was a staggering £11,000. In 1846 whale oil cost between five and eight shillings per gallon, a heavy drain on the often stretched resources of lighthouse authorities.

About that time colza oil, derived from a variant of the plant which produces Swedish turnips, began to take over. A close relative to the rapeseed plant, it was grown extensively in France, Belgium, Holland and Germany. At two shillings and nine pence per gallon it was much more economical than sperm whale oil. In other parts of the world, olive oil, lard oil and coconut oil were burned in lighthouse and lightship lamps. When a lighthouse was built on Cape Sierra Leone, West Africa in the 1840s, to warn shipping of the Carpenter Rocks, the oil burned in its lamps was extracted under pressure from locally-grown ground nuts. Mineral oil was first employed in 1865 in a multi-wick burner invented by a Captain Doty. The oils could be petroleum, Scottish shale oil or paraffin, any of which could be bought for just a fraction of the cost of vegetable oils.

The next major breakthrough in lightship illuminants before the evolution of the electric plant aboard ship came with the bright, clean flame produced by acetylene gas. This product, which could be stored under pressure, also made practical for the first time the widespread use of unmanned light vessels.

LIGHT BITES

An unnamed seaman, while serving on the *Swin Middle* Lightship in the Thames estuary in 1922 said, 'For the operation of the foghorn we used a gas-oil engine by Hornsby Ackroyd which, after you eventually got it started, was kept going only by the unholy cussing it received. While you operated the foghorn you received an extra penny an hour to be divided by all on board for that month. This was the only 'perk' you could expect on top of the wages of £3.5s. a week.' Excerpt from *The Uniform* magazine of May, 1965.

In 1837 the lightship at Swin Middle became the first ever to be fitted with a revolving light.

In December, 1929, during the time of alcohol prohibition in Finland, a rum-running boat with a cargo full of contraband spirits almost rammed the lightship *Relanderinmatala*. A last-gasp change of course by the booze cruiser managed to avoid a potentially explosive collision. The lightship carried several names through-out her long career and is now a major exhibit at the maritime museum in Helsinki.

In a report in the early 1840s on Trinity House light vessels, Captain Washington, RN argued that one reason for the frequent loss of station by these ships was the severity of the Admiralty test for mooring chains. After such a test, a second trial found the cables able to bear only half the strain registered in the first test. Another reason may have been that the chain was not well made in the first place for the chain-making industry of the 19th century had more than its fair share of 'cowboys'. The *Shipping and Mercantile Gazette* of December 27th,1862 made a chilling point. Of 523 shipping casualties around the coast of Britain in the course of a single week, 190 occurred through faulty anchors and cables. The Liverpool Corporation's cable-proving equipment showed that 82.25% of 'merchant ship quality' chain failed at a proof strain of well below 11 tons. Even though lightship chain was of a higher quality – the weight of the ship was doubled or trebled during calculations to assess the strength of chain needed – cables still parted with depressing regularity.

LV 90
(South Goodwin)

*T*he Strait of Dover is the busiest international waterway in the world. At the eastern end of the English Channel, this tightest of gaps between England and France hums with activity. Up to 500 vessels pour through the Strait every 24 hours – even more at the height of the ferry sailings season in August. In 1993, through traffic amounted to a stupendous 3.8 billion tons deadweight.

Impressive as this is, the mind reels at what it must have been like in the later years of the 19th century, with Britain at the hub of the biggest empire the world has ever seen. In terms of numbers of vessels, consideration must be given to the distribution of cargo aboard one container ship today among perhaps 20 ships 150 years ago. To this flurry of merchantmen pouring in from across the globe add the huge coastal trade that carried everything of any bulk in the absence of good roads. Add further the swarming fishing fleets of the Channel harbours. Add the trade of the countries of northern Europe whose major outlet to the Atlantic was the English Channel and some notion of scale begins to emerge.

Picture a vessel of that time, say an East Indiaman, joining this jungle of sails on the very last leg of a voyage from the Far East. The Thames and London beckon. Wives and sweethearts are barely a hug away. Yet here it is that these homesick sailors, armed with crude navigation equipment and at the mercy of the fickle wind, encounter the Goodwin Sands. The most feared of all marine hazards, it's as though the Devil himself had placed the sands where they could reap the richest harvest of lives.

On calm summer days, they present a benign enough aspect. At low water, picnics would be held upon them and ball games played. But let the tide creep across the sand and the wind begin to exercise its lungs, then the Goodwins grin and bare their teeth. Thirty-five square miles of shifting sand, peat, ooze and rotting wood from the trees that flourished there in the days before the sea rushed in and swamped the land. Situated about six miles offshore between the North and South Forelands, the Goodwins straddle the strait. The depth of sand measures fully 80 feet before reaching a bed of ancient chalk. Thousands of vessels lie buried there. Viking long-ships, liners, galleons, tugs, yachts, trawlers, traders of every size and nationality – and a lightship. The destructive power of the Goodwins was reflected in a Board of Trade return for the years 1851–1862 inclusive. This showed 17 wrecks on the sands resulting in loss of life, not including collisions. In two cases the number of casualties was unknown. In the remaining 15 wrecks 89 people died.

The *South Goodwin* Lightship station was established as the South Sand Head in 1832, five miles off South Foreland. She joined two other vessels as the first pearls in what was to become a glowing necklace of lightships and gas buoys thrown around the sands.

The *South Goodwin* was the most vulnerable of all the ships marking the area. Facing the prevailing south-westerlies, she was in danger of being blown onto the sands in the event of a problem with her mooring. But it was Man, not Mother Nature, who conspired to bring about the first *South Goodwin* loss. During the Second World War, *LV 69* was sunk by enemy action on October 21st, 1940. The ship, luckily, had been converted to unattended function and the crew withdrawn.

In the history of the *South Goodwin* station however, this is not the first date that comes to mind. Neither is Christmas, 1899 when the lightship broke adrift; Christmas 1914 when the same thing happened; nor March 24th, 1929 when a German steamship rammed the light vessel, causing major damage.

The year etched indelibly on the brain is 1954.

As the month of November drew towards its close, the weather in the Channel worsened. By the 26th, a full gale was blowing from the south-south-west. So severe was the storm that further along the Channel, the 82,000-ton liner *Queen Mary* elected to delay her scheduled departure from Southampton to New York.

Around the Goodwins, three lightships were riding out the storm – *South Goodwin*, *East Goodwin* and *North Goodwin*. As darkness fell on the 26th, the wind increased to hurricane force, frequently exceeding Force 11 on the Beaufort scale. Even in Dover harbour, a 12-foot swell was running.

As if the wind were not enough, *LV 90* (*South Goodwin*) was also having to contend with a fierce tide racing in the same direction through the strait. The combined weight of wind and tide that night was beyond description. In his quarter of a century in the lightship service, 49-year-old Tom Skipp, Master of the *South Goodwin*, could recall nothing like it.

Skipp was a worried man. Armed with a torch, he prowled the length of his ship making certain that all was secure, even risking his life to venture onto the fore-deck which was being swept by huge waves, to examine the riding cable. As with all light-ship cables it was of exceptional strength, in this case 210 fathoms (about 410 metres) of 1 inch Tayco steel chain connecting the ship with her four-ton Martin anchor.

With difficulty the Master checked his position with the South Foreland light, which was often obscured entirely by rain squalls. All seemed well enough.

Sharing Skipp's cabin, on an assignment from the Ministry of Agriculture and Fisheries, was 22-year-old Ronald Keir Murton. His mission was pest control, logging the flight patterns of wood pigeons. He was the only non-professional seaman among the crew and had been on board for a month.

Murton had turned in early although not with any hope of sleep. The pitching and rolling of the lightship rendered this natural function quite impractical. But the violent motion was as the rocking of a cradle compared with what was to come. The *South Goodwin* buried her nose into a tremendous sea and the ship staggered under the weight of it. Much to Murton's alarm, some water forced its way into the cabin. He grabbed a cardigan, pulled it over his pyjamas and went up to the lookout shelter to join the two men on watch. It was 11 pm.

Tom Skipp again checked the ship's position by compass and was apparently satisfied although there was now some unease about the riding cable which seemed to have little strain upon it. There is no means of establishing the exact moment but it appears that sometime between midnight and 1 am the anchor cable had parted. *LV 90* was now being driven towards the sands.

At the Coastguard stations at Deal and Ramsgate, there was a growing sense that something was wrong. At 01:03, the Ramsgate log reports no sign of either the *South* or *East Goodwin* lightships, although the log acknowledges poor visibility. The Deal Coastguard staff were convinced that either of the lightships, or some other vessel, was adrift and setting north-east.

Ramsgate called both lightships but got no reply. By 0108 the coxswain of the Ramsgate lifeboat was contacted but, quite correctly, in the absence of definite evidence of a ship in distress, he was not prepared to launch.

Aboard the *South Goodwin*, in a moment of improved visibility, the ship was suddenly bathed in light. They were almost alongside *LV 12*, the *East Goodwin* Lightship! Only now did the awful truth strike home. They were miles off station. The *East Goodwin* crew could only watch in horror as their sister ship swept by.

Murton offered to rouse those crewmen who were off duty and ran to awaken the three men in the crew's quarters. Not surprisingly, none was asleep. They made their way to the galley. All the crew were now in this part of the ship, except for one man in the lookout shelter.

Ashore, there was now no doubt about the emergency. The *East Goodwin* had radioed in: '*South Goodwin* Lightship adrift and nearly on sands abeam of us'.

At 01:28, maroons were fired at Walmer and Ramsgate to assemble the lifeboat crews there. Dover lifeboat also made ready for sea. At Ramsgate, some crewmen had not heard the crack of the maroons because of the storm and the lifeboat's assistant mechanic had to run around on his motor bike knocking them up. The maroons were fired a second time.

By 02:42 the lifeboat was at sea, her full crew complement on board. At Walmer, the lifeboat was ready to go but could not launch because of a shelf of fine shingle built up by the pounding waves in front of the launching platform. The crew fell frantically to shovelling this away as the tide ebbed but by the time they were ready to launch, the decision was taken to hold the boat in reserve since both Dover and Ramsgate lifeboats were now out searching for the lightship.

But disaster had already overtaken the crew of *LV 90*. No sooner had they assembled in the galley than the ship piled onto the sands, collapsing onto her starboard side. Some of the men received burns, thrown onto the coal-fired stove before water flooded into the compartment, dousing the fire. The lightship had struck in the Kellet Gut area of the sands about 1.30 am, having been driven 6½ miles.

Inside the galley, the men were fighting for survival. Pots and pans and other cooking items were swirling around in the water, crashing into them. The door was under water, sealing off the exit. There was just one way out – the skylight, which had been broken by the impact. Time and again the men tried to reach it, often being beaten back by water cascading through it.

Finally Murton, the youngest man aboard, managed to grasp the skylight frame and dragged himself through. In so doing, he succeeded only in exchanging one nightmare for another. He was now clinging on to the near-vertical deckhouse roof, being battered by seas thundering over the sands. He could hear the men in the galley and the lookout in his cabin and tried to communicate with them but his voice was wrenched away in the fury of the storm.

Murton was also in grave peril from one of the ship's lifeboats thrashing about just above him. It was essential he got to a safer position and he set himself to crawl to the port boat deck handrail near the base of the lantern tower. He managed to entwine his arms and legs through it. Now, somehow, through the eternity of that awful night, he had to hold out until help arrived.

LV 90 was not located until daylight, nearly two miles north by north-east of the *East Goodwin* Lightship. The Ramsgate lifeboat closed to about 150 yards but could see no sign of life. It was impossible to get closer.

The end of *LV 90*.
Daily Express syndicated photograph.

At the RAF base at Manston, a reconnaissance flight of the United States Air Force's 66th Air Rescue Squadron took off at 7.30 am. In their Grumman Albatross S.A. 16 amphibian, the crew made several runs over the ship. They saw no sign of life.

Murton, who had heard the aircraft, was now undergoing the worst moments of his ordeal. He had detected a faint tapping from inside the hull. Painfully, he crawled towards the noise which seemed to be coming from behind a skylight at the after end of the deckhouse above the crew's quarters. He called out and was answered by crewman Ben Porter, who told him that Tom Skipp and fog signal driver Walter Viney were with him, both in a bad way.

Porter said he was all right but 'jolly hungry'. He asked if Murton could open the skylight. Try as he might, the exhausted man simply could not unscrew the nuts holding it in place. He shouted that help was on its way and managed to regain his position on the rail.

Back at Manston the feeling was one of hopelessness but the Americans were unwilling to give up, despite a communications nightmare resulting from their squadron antenna being destroyed by the gale.

The crew of a Sikorsky H-19 rescue helicopter volunteered to take a look. In conditions which were really beyond the margins for the aircraft the pilot, Captain Curtiss E. Parkins and his crew, medic Elmer Vollman and co-pilot Major Paul Parks, took off and reached the wreck just after 9 a.m. The Walmer lifeboat was also in attendance.

That Ronald Murton was still alive was due to the fact that for most of his time clinging to his rail the tide had been falling. However, it was on the flood again when the helicopter arrived. When he heard the clatter of the engine, Murton looked up but could see nothing. He was later to describe a kind of fog obscuring his vision. In fact his eyes were clogged with salt and sand. In the Sikorsky, the Americans were riding their luck. They dropped so close to the stricken lightship that spray was coming into the cabin.

They could hardly believe their eyes. Looking up at them was a man. A survivor! Quickly they lowered a sling but Murton could not see it. Hovering was proving very difficult in the 40-knot winds and there was a real danger of the rescue line snagging on wreckage. If that happened, Captain Parkins would have had no choice but to ditch the line to save his aircraft, leaving Murton to his fate.

Parkins again manoeuvred until the sling actually bumped against the man on the rail. Now Murton was able to pass his legs through it. 30 seconds later he was aboard the helicopter – the rescue operation had taken just three minutes. For close on eight hours, Murton had survived the worst winter storm to hit the Channel in half a century, clad only in pyjamas and a cardigan.

His first words were for his fellow crewmen, still alive in the hull and even as Murton was being flown to Manston, the first stages of a rescue operation were being mapped out. It was a race against time that was always going to be lost.

Even as another Sikorsky was preparing to get airborne from Manston with cutting equipment, 15 miles to the south-east the rising tide was covering the *South Goodwin*. By noon, a full hour before high water, she was completely submerged.

Left: Survivor being winched up from the *South Goodwin*.
Daily Express syndicated photograph.

The wreckage of the *South Goodwin* minutes after the survivor was rescued.
Daily Express syndicated photograph.

The wind, which had dropped to about 35 mph early in the day, was again blowing a full gale. The rescue operation had to be suspended.

Even in those darkest of moments, the importance of the lightship station was not forgotten and the name *South Goodwin* was already being painted on the sides of a spare lightship at Harwich, *LV 65*, as she was made ready for sea to take the place of her doomed sister. A temporary lighted bell buoy was laid by 7 pm on Saturday the 27th, removed when *LV 65* got into position on the 29th.

Not until the Sunday could divers get aboard the wreck. There was no trace of the crew. Even during a fuller search the following day all they found inside was sand. Not a single body was recovered. However, not everyone may have been trapped inside the ship. There was some evidence to suggest that crew members may have managed to reach the deck and launch a Carley life-raft.

LV 90 had already settled four to five feet into the sand as the Goodwins set about devouring their latest victim. The ship did not disappear entirely however and at low tide, traces of her can still be seen today.

Captain Parkins became the first airman to receive the silver medal of the Royal National Lifeboat Institution, presented by the Duchess of Kent, for the courageous rescue of Ronald Murton. Medical technician Vollman and co-pilot Park were awarded bronze medals at the ceremony on March 8th, 1955.

A disaster relief fund was set up for the dependants of the crew. At the launch of the fund, a joint statement from the mayors of Deal and Ramsgate read:

> *To many, the presence of the light and the work and patience of the men who manned the ship is taken as a matter of course and it is only when there is such a disaster as has now overtaken its crew that attention is focused upon the hazardous life which they lead. Thousands of voyagers have passed safely by the notorious Goodwin Sands by reason of the presence of the lightship.*
>
>   Amen to that.

The work of the *South Goodwin* Lightship station goes on. In place of *LV 90*, the spare lightship from Harwich was towed into position. When it was later replaced by *LV 17*, this lightship was given a five-ton Byers anchor, the biggest type employed on British lightships.

At the time of writing, the number of lightships around the British coast is down to single figures, the *South Goodwin* being one of them. It was fully automated in 1985 and is permanently monitored by telemetry link from North Foreland Lighthouse.

At one stage, including Ireland, there were more than 60 manned light vessels serving the mariner around the British Isles. Including unattended lightships, the figure in 1910 was actually 87. It was easily the biggest lightship fleet in the world.

LIGHT BITES

The German lightship occupying the Elbe 1 station in 1979 took delivery of 20 survival suits on March 8th. The crew were required to wear them on deck during heavy weather. On March 27th, one seaman fell overboard wearing a suit. He survived.

A few retired light vessels serve today as bases for amateur radio stations. Such a one is *LV XXI*, part of the maritime museum complex at Ebeltoft, Denmark, displaying government-built wooden ships in former public service. The original radio sets on board have been modified to allow the operators to use 'ham' frequencies. Call sign of the station is OZ7DAL. It has a worldwide range. *LV XXI* was launched on August 15th, 1911. Like every Danish lightship bar one, she was built of wood.

The case of the French lightship *Ruytingen 1890* was a curious one – she actually went missing for eight years. Considered to be unserviceable in 1939, she was transferred to Government control on December 11th with the recommendation that she be scrapped. In the confusion that followed the invasion and occupation of France by the Third Reich in 1940, the ship disappeared. In 1947, two years after the war ended, the French lighthouse authorities re-discovered the ship berthed close to a lock in the harbour of Antwerp, Belgium. The hull had been reinforced and anti-aircraft turrets installed on deck. The French Consul in Antwerp was instructed to get rid of the ship and she was sold for scrap where she lay.

With the invention in 1822 by French physicist Augustin-Jean Fresnel of an efficient lens system for lighthouses and lightships, the oil-fired lamps then used were able to generate much higher power. However, the arrangement occasionally backfired. During summer, when the sun shone through the lantern and then the lens, enough heat could be produced to ignite the wicks in the lamps. To get round this, lightkeepers would sometimes drape a cloth or blanket over the lens during daylight.

LS 82
(Buffalo)

*T*he Great Lakes which mark part of the border between the United States and Canada combine to create easily the greatest single surface area of fresh water on Earth – 96,000 square miles of it. For the ships that sail these five inland waterways, certain problems apply which are not met in the wide oceans. Difficult as it is to believe, by far the highest reading on any ship's strain gauge was taken aboard the *Edward L. Ryerson* on Lake Michigan during the storm of November, 1966. A reading of 23,000 lbs per square inch was recorded. There is no record of an ocean-going vessel beginning to approach that level of stress. Part of the reason may lie in the short, steep waves produced by storms on the lakes. Their battering of hulls comes in a succession of rapid blows, like combination punches from a boxer.

Ice has been known to freeze the entire lakes area, even persisting in places until June. This would sometimes lead to such a rapid build-up of ice on superstructures that ships became unstable in a matter of minutes and overturned.

The relative lack of buoyancy of the fresh water was an added danger and may be the principal reason for the grim reputation of the lakes for refusing to give up their dead. At one time the lakes had seven working lightships. The first three lightships built in 1891 with propulsion power in America were designed for use during the navigation season there.

LS 82 came later, built at Muskegon, Michigan, in 1912. As was normal for the lakes, she was smaller than sea-going lightships. For this reason, lakes lightships could not carry standard one-ton lanterns at their mastheads. They were given much lighter lens lanterns of which they sometimes carried three, one for each mast. Total weight for three such lanterns was just 700 lbs (320 kilograms).

An unusual feature of *LS 82* was a cover for the foredeck in the shape of a whaleback, thought ideal protection against waves crashing over the bow. She carried a wide range of fog-signalling equipment – a big bell on the foredeck, a six-inch steam whistle on the funnel, a submarine bell and hand bell. Her crew comprised

LS 82 under way. Note the large mushroom anchor at the bow and the black oval meshed screen at the masthead – her daymark.
Photograph courtesy of J. Clary, from *Ladies of the Lakes II*, Altwerger and Mandel Publishing Company.

four officers and two seamen. Among the comforts they enjoyed on board were leather-upholstered oak chairs, French plate glass mirrors and a small library.

They were to have the honour of establishing the *Buffalo* light vessel station at the eastern edge of Lake Erie, close by the Niagara River and Buffalo harbour. The mushroom-shaped anchor of *LS 82* first hit the bottom on August 3rd, 1912. Her assignment was supposed to be temporary, due to last only until the completion of *LS 96*, at that time still under construction. Her precise position was 13 miles west of Buffalo, off Point Albino, Canada. In addition to steering ships away from the shoals along the Canadian coast, she marked the potentially dangerous wreck of the steamer *W.C. Richardson*.

November has an especial reputation for evil weather on the lakes. But the storm that struck in early November, 1913, was the worst since meteorological data began to be kept. A record low barometric pressure reading was taken at Erie, Pennsylvania, on the southern shore of the lake, 75 miles from the lightship on November 9th. The area covered by the storm was massive and eight ships were lost in Lake Huron, 150 miles from Erie. In total, 12 ships went down and 200 lives were lost.

The lights of *LS 82* were last seen at 4.45 am on Monday the 10th. The loss of the lightship was not suspected however, until the Tuesday, when a lifebelt from the ship and some debris were found inside the breakwater at Buffalo. The lightship tender vessel *Crocus* and the tug *Yale* set out to seek more pointers to the fate of the lightship. There was still some hope that she might have survived, perhaps beached somewhere. It was reasoned that the material discovered could have been washed off the deck.

That hope was soon dashed. Further items began to turn up, including a brass petrol tank cover and, shockingly, a wooden hatch cover upon which were scrawled the words: *Goodbye Nellie... Ship is breaking up fast ...Williams.*

The chilling message contained not just a portent of imminent disaster but a riddle as well. Captain Hugh McClennan Williams had promised his wife that he would leave some kind of note if danger threatened. But Mrs Williams, whom he had never called Nellie, was convinced he had not written the note. And why would a husband sign such a note only with his surname?

In any event, Mrs Williams refused to give up hope. She spent two days aboard the *Crocus* as the ship scoured the lake in a vain search for survivors. Years afterwards, Mrs Williams came to the view that her husband, perhaps injured, had asked another member of the crew to write a note for him.

LS 82, the *Buffalo*, during the storm that drove her to the bottom of Lake Erie.
Painting reproduced courtesy of J. Clary from *Ladies of the Lakes II*, Altwerger and Mandel Publishing Company.

It was a year before the only body was found, that of Chief Engineer Charles Butler. In the chilly fresh water it was almost perfectly preserved. The ship itself was finally located in May, 1914. The search vessel *Surveyor* found the wreck in 62 feet of water two miles from her station. A diver reported that the storm had parted the ship's anchor cable and battered in its superstructure before swamping it.

On September 16th, 1915, the Reid Wrecking and Towing Company raised the ship. *LS 82* was completely refitted at Detroit and actually resumed her career as a light vessel. After many years of faithful service she was scrapped in 1945.

The wreck of *LS 82*, raised on September 16th, 1915. From *Ladies of the Lakes II*, J. Clary. Photograph by permission of J. Clary from *Ladies of the Lakes II*, Altwerger and Mandel Publishing Company.

LV Storbrotten

Mines were a constant hazard to lightships – and not just in wartime. During both the First and Second World Wars, there were so many mines in the North Sea that the Danish Lights and Buoys Service withdrew all the lightships from their west coast stations.

On December 28th, 1914, a storm from the south-east parted the English light-ship, the *South Sand Head*, from its anchor. The crew were a great deal luckier than they had any right to expect. Not only did the ship contrive to avoid the Goodwin Sands but she was blown right through a minefield before anchoring safely near Margate.

Early in 1916, the *East Goodwin* Lightship parted her mooring in bad weather. Before a spare anchor could be used, this ship too had drifted into a minefield. The Master of the Trinity House vessel *Vestal* decided to go in after the lightship, crank-ing up his engine to maximum revolutions in the hope that the *Vestal's* bow wave would push any mines out of the way. The crew, all wearing lifejackets, were kept standing by the lifeboats. Fortune decided to favour the brave and the *East Goodwin* was taken in tow to Margate Roads where a new anchor and cable were supplied and she was returned to her station. For the crews of both ships the four hours they spent in the minefield must have been the longest of their lives.

In the English Channel during the Second World War, the crew of the *North Sand Head* Lightship (later renamed *North Goodwin*) spotted a mine floating towards them. They used the tiller bar in an attempt to wrestle their ship out of the way but without success. The mine dipped into their bow before floating harmlessly away, one of its horns badly bent.

The crew of the *Gull* Lightship frequently saw drifting mines and witnessed a number of ships being damaged by them. The French lightship *Sandettie* 1937 was totally destroyed by a mine off La Pallice in the Bay of Biscay on November 4th, 1942.

British lightships were sometimes employed as mine-watchers and carried out such duties in the River Orwell and in the Thames, where *LV 64* was assigned to the

Flying the 'red duster', the light vessel *Juno* in her wartime role as a guide to the Normandy invasion forces. Painting reproduced courtesy of Trinity House.

task at Sea Reach. However, the crews were not given rifles to shoot mines, as were the keepers of 16 selected lighthouses around the British Isles. This odd move followed the severe damage inflicted by a mine on the Tuskar Rock lighthouse on the Irish coast on December 2nd, 1941.

During the Normandy landings of 1944, two Trinity House lightships, *LV 72* carrying the name *Juno* and another named *Kansas*, marked a lane through a minefield. Between these bobbing gateposts surged the greatest armada the world had ever seen. *Juno* and *Kansas* trembled for hours as the big guns of the Allied fleet pounded German defences on the Normandy coastline.

In Finnish waters, the lightships encountered major problems with mines in the aftermath of the 1914–18 war. Here lay particular difficulties, not only of numbers but of types. Both the Germans and the Russians had sown thousands of mines. Work on clearing them began at the end of the war and continued until 1924. However, in the Aland Sea between Finland and Sweden, operations were concluded in 1921 and the lightship *Storbrotten* sailed out in the autumn of that year to resume her task of marking the Storbrotten Rocks, north of the Aland Islands. It soon became clear that the mine-clearing operations had been concluded too quickly for mines continued to be reported in the area, almost on a daily basis.

On September 16th, 1922, the crew of the *Storbrotten* spotted a mine close by. They managed to stop it drifting away and secured it to a rope, leaving the device bobbing well astern. The staff of the pilot district at Marianhamn were informed and they ordered the inspection vessel *Walvoja* to go to the scene and tow the mine away to be destroyed. This course of action was crucially delayed by a sudden storm.

The Master of the lightship was himself in Marianhamn with two of his seamen at that time, collecting supplies. They were not able to set out on a return voyage to the ship until September 21st, although the weather was still poor. They came to within a mile of the lightship when there was a tremendous explosion. Smoke was seen pouring from the stern of the *Storbrotten* and she quickly disappeared from sight.

It was thought at first that all on board had been killed. In fact, one seaman had managed to swim to a nearby islet and he was able to reveal that the mine had drifted into the ship's stern. Six crewmen died. The *Storbrotten* was replaced by lightship *Reserv 1* within days.

Footnote: Finland's lightships were always withdrawn at the onset of winter and resumed work in the spring. Finland is the only country in the world which has all of its harbours frozen in during winter. This led to famine in the winter of 1867–68, well before the establishment of a rail link between Russia and Finland. A crop failure was followed by conditions so severe that it was late May before grain ships could enter Finnish ports. By that time more than 110,000 people had died of cold and starvation.

LIGHT BITES

The last lightship to serve upon the Columbia station off the Columbia River, Oregon, is in the care of the Columbia River Maritime Museum. Over the winter of 1983/84, a class of diesel mechanics took on the lightship as a project and began to bring her engines back to life. Included in the class was a grandmother, June McClure, who was beginning a new career as a marine engineer. As a result of their efforts and of other volunteers, the lightship was able to sail upriver to Portland for that town's Maritime Festival in the summer of 1984. She ran smoothly and almost reached her 1950 sea trials speed.

The *Columbia* lightship at her mooring at Astoria, Oregon.

BF 7
(Ruytingen 1938)

*T*he French lightship service, having remained unmolested during the First
World War, was severely depleted during the second.

Ruytingen 1938 was so named because her construction was completed in that
year. Her official designation was *Bateau Feu 7*. The task of the ship was to mark the
channel between the Out-Ruytingen and In-Ruytingen sandbanks in the shallow
approaches to Dunkirk. Several vessels had occupied this station since its creation
in 1863. The area was very exposed and the moorings of the lightships had parted
several times.

However, on the outbreak of war in September, 1939, the new ship found
herself on the *Dyck* station, some way to the south-west, signalling the entrance to
the narrow West Pass through the maze of the Flemish sandbanks. Her 3000-watt
light was reduced to 500 watts, decreasing its range from 17 to five nautical miles.(A
nautical mile equals one minute of longitude measured along the Equator. Its length
is 6,082.66 feet, almost exactly 250 metres longer than a land mile.) Immediately,
the lightship became involved in hostilities.

On September 9th the crew were able to rescue four aviators from a British plane
which had crashed into the sea nearby. On September 16th, they rescued the
survivors from the wreck of the British cargo carrier *Bramden*. On December 8th the
French lightshipmen started their engine and slipped their cable to go to the rescue
of seamen from the oil tanker *British Liberty* which had struck a line of mines and
gone up in flames. The tanker was drifting towards more mines when the rescue took
place. The brave lightship crew saved 17 men from certain death that day.

The charmed life of their ship did not last much longer. *Ruytingen 1938* paid the
ultimate price for staying doggedly at her very high risk station when, on May 25th,
1940, she was attacked by a Junkers 88 bomber and sunk. The lightship crew were
all picked up safely by the trawler *Joseph Marie*. Three more French light vessels were
lost before the war ended in 1945.

The Sandettie Lightship station carved out its own tiny piece of lightship history by exchanging nationalities. With the introduction in 1987 of the Territorial Waters Act, which increased British territorial waters from three to 12 miles, the French station became British. Here, *Bateau Feu 6* is guarding the shoal.

France's only peacetime lightship disaster occurred in 1933. A new lightship, the *Dunkerque*, had temporarily acquired the name *Dyck* and was manning that station while the real *Dyck* was in dry dock, undergoing repairs.

On December 13th, in the course of a biting easterly gale, the cable broke at the mooring ring. The lightship began to lurch and roll like a drunk in the street and had been adrift in rough seas for about three quarters of a nautical mile before a standby anchor could be used. When this chain also snapped, the ship heeled over, turned broadside to the waves and grounded near the Gravelines lighthouse a few kilometres east of Calais. Listing heavily to starboard, she began to suffer a severe pounding from waves dashing onto the rocks.

A rescue could not be effected because of the position of the ship and the severity of the weather. Captain Francois Huysman and crewmen Francois Hars, Jerome Dewaele and Leopold Goetghebeur drowned in the freezing water. The tragedy triggered a spontaneous outburst of sympathy from the French public and a benefit concert was held on February 4th, 1934 for the bereaved families.

LV 19
(Halifax)

When the ranks of platers, gangers and riveters assembled to witness yet another launch of their handiwork from the Paisley shipyard of Bow and McLachlan and Co. Ltd. in February, 1914, there was much shaking of caps, perched as they were upon heads steeped in the superstitions attending ships and shipbuilding.

For to add to the instinctive disposition of these Scots in the direction of doom and gloom was the date of the launch – Friday the 13th. Even the weather conspired to support the mood of pessimism. A full gale was blowing from the south-west with near-horizontal showers drenching the onlookers. A huge tide filled the River Cart to bursting point and there was some flooding on the Clyde – of which the Cart was a tributary – notably at Helensburgh.

The naming ceremony was performed by Mrs J.J. Ferguson, wife of the Canadian Government ship surveyor under whose authority the ship was built. Among others on the VIP platform that day were Captain and Mrs Farquhar of Halifax, Nova Scotia; Mr French, principal surveyor of Lloyds and his colleague from Glasgow, Mr Minchin.

The Clyde was not just the busiest stretch of shipbuilding water in the world – it was unarguably the best. And it was familiar territory for the Canadians, who had a tradition of ordering ships from Paisley yards in particular. It was usually Fleming & Ferguson who managed to undercut everyone else and they built up great experience in producing icebreakers and lighthouse tenders for their overseas customers. But the sales team from the triangular-shaped Bow McLachlan yard three miles south of the Clyde had managed to land the latest contract. It was their first and last Canadian order.

The company practised an expertise that was typical of this noisy, vibrant power-house of heavy industry. They even made their own cranes and the machinery for their foundry. In the boiler shop, boiler plate 1⅝ inches thick could be riveted.

Trading countries clamoured to buy ships bearing the proud adjective 'Clyde-built', despite a recent history of poor labour relations in the industry – early rumblings of the full-blown unrest which followed the Bolshevik revolution of 1917 and was eventually to earn the river the nickname Red Clydeside. Now, however, as Europe slid inexorably towards the war to end all wars, seamen found frequent employment taking a steady stream of newly-completed ships to owners all over the globe. Such a vessel was the latest product from Bow and McLachlan.

Built to enter the service of the Canadian Coastguard, she was a lightship, designated *Halifax No 19* and set to shine her oil-fired lights off Sambro Point in the approaches to Halifax, Nova Scotia. Self-propelled, she was scheduled to cross the Atlantic in April, bound for Halifax where she would receive most of her operating equipment.

Lightships being by the nature of their work mostly stationary, no-one could have been surprised if this were to be her one move of any significance. But when the 135-foot ship did finally put out from the Broomielaw on the Clyde on April 21st, the fates had already decreed it was also to be her last.

Yet she was in good hands. Master of the vessel was Captain John McBeath, of Partick, Glasgow. In his mid-60s, Captain McBeath was one of the most highly thought of master mariners on the Clyde. His area of expertise was in the delivery of new ships to shipyard customers wherever they might be. Even the mate, John Anderson, was a former master so there was experience aplenty on board. Another Glasgow man, he was also well-known in Dundee where he had spent many years.

The rest of the crew – all Scots bar one – consisted of three engineers, four firemen (stokers), a cook and William Morrison, described in the crew list simply as 'boy'. They had a fine new ship under them, the broad ocean before them and a landfall in Halifax about a month away.

From the start they had bad luck. After a brief call at Queenstown, Ireland, their Atlantic crossing proved extremely rough with much heavy ice encountered. The ship rode the conditions well but used far more coal than anticipated. Captain McBeath was compelled to put into St John's, Newfoundland to replenish the bunkers. They spent two days there before setting off on the final 500 nautical miles of their voyage to Halifax. But what waited to undo the ship off the Nova Scotia coast was the very reason she was going there – fog.

Like many another lightship, *Halifax No 19* was to have had at least equal importance as a fog signal station in an area plagued by that most unnerving of sea conditions. And on Friday, May 22nd, the ship found herself ensnared by it. Although she was equipped with the latest wireless telephone apparatus, this was not operational. Along with the other gear awaiting her arrival in the dockyard at Halifax was a vital radio part which would complete that installation.

As *Halifax No 19* tiptoed through the murk with still 100 miles to go, there was little wind but a heavy sea was running. Fishermen working the area heard a fog whistle about 4 pm and it continued to sound intermittently until 10 pm. The locals were familiar with the fog signals of most vessels plying their patch but this was the voice of a stranger. There seems little doubt that what they heard was the secondary fog signal of the lightship – a large organ whistle fitted to the funnel. Whether it was or not the fishermen were concerned that a steamer should be so close to Liscomb Island in such thick weather.

The enforced stop-over at St John's had done the lightship no favours, placing her well off the recommended track from Scotland to Halifax. And when she finally came to grief she was 30 miles north of that route. News of the fate which had over-taken *Halifax No 19* first came in a message from Liscomb on May 23rd. Captain Murdoch of the steamer *Dufferin* reported picking up three bodies wearing lifebelts marked *Halifax 19*. They were floating in water strewn with debris including tables, chairs and bedding. Doubtless a shiver accompanied Captain Murdoch's report that the dead men still had colour in their cheeks.

That same day the lightship was found, bottom up, on a reef known as Crook's Ledge, jutting out from Liscomb Island four miles short of Liscomb Harbour. Six more badly-battered bodies were recovered and two smashed lifeboats. Local opinion held that *Halifax No 19* had grounded on an outer reef, Long Ledge (the wreck had been found, queerly, by a fisherman called Long) and had been carried by the huge swell onto Crook's Ledge. The shoreline of the island was littered with wreckage.

Captain Blois of the Government steamer *Stanley* had been off Halifax awaiting the arrival of the new lightship, ready to escort her into port. Now he was instructed to make for the scene at full speed and arrived about 8 pm on the Saturday. There was little he could do that night but dawn delivered a bright spring Sunday and he was able to report that the lightship lay in two parts, almost totally submerged. Insured for £26,000, she was a complete write-off.

Marine engineers from the Canadian capital of Ottawa arrived at the scene and concluded that the sea must have been running very high to wreck such a strong vessel so comprehensively. They noted her extra large frames and scantlings, her large bow, the great width of the ship at the waterline with the sides inclining inwards and upwards towards the deck. They also saw that the lifeboats' tackle was cut away, indicating that at least some of the crew had escaped the dying ship. The inspectors reasoned that the lifeboats had capsized among the breakers on the rocks, killing rather than drowning their occupants. The eventual recovery of the ship's chrono-meter almost certainly fixed the time of the first thunderous impact with the reef. It had stopped at 10.20 local time (2.20 pm GMT).

With the loss of *Halifax No 19* and her crew, the flinty ledges off Liscomb had re-established what was already a grim reputation. Fifteen years before, the steamer *Ealing* was lost there, drowning 15. The Allan Line steamer *Indian* piled up on the same rocks in 1864, 30 lives being lost on that occasion. And the newly-dug graves of six of the lightship's crew were just yards from those interred victims of a British brigantine which went down with all hands in 1884.

But it was the loss of the lightship which echoed with a terrible irony. Sent from Old Scotland to safeguard shipping on the fog-bound coast of New Scotland, she became its immediate victim. By this unhappy twist of fate she carved for herself a sad niche in the history of the service. Of a certainty she stands alone as the light-ship which perished at her place of employment before she could serve so much as a single day.

On May 22nd, 1973, on the 59th anniversary of the disaster, a monument was erected in the tiny cemetery of the United Church at Liscomb to mark the graves of those Scots who had died so far from home. It stands just 60 miles from the town of New Glasgow. Chiselled into its stonework are the words:

> *In memory of the Master and Crew of the Halifax Lightship No. 19 wrecked off Liscomb 22 May, 1914 with the loss of all on board. Those given up by the sea here found eternal rest.*

A maritime disaster without survivors has the habit of throwing up a number of unanswered questions. In the case of *Halifax No 19*, the principal of those and still a mystery today, was: who was the 'Passenger to Louisburg'? During the search which followed the accident, some women's clothing and a child's sock were found. And a trunk. The name upon it was indecipherable but the words 'Passenger to Louisburg' were clear enough. Extensive inquiries at Queenstown, St John's and back in Glasgow revealed that no passenger had embarked on the lightship at any of these places.

The waterside community of Louisburg, 100 miles east of Liscomb on Cape Breton Island, had provided Canada with its first-ever lighthouse, built by the French in 1773. No one there came forward to inquire about a missing woman or child. The reach of the inquiry extended as far as Louisburg, North Carolina and still drew a blank. Since the only bodies ever found were those of adult males, the evidence that a woman and child were on board seems sketchy.

But it's impossible to write off entirely a connection with *Halifax No 19*. Was Captain McBeath carrying unauthorised passengers? Could he even have been attempting to land a passenger at Liscomb rather than face an awkward interrogation at Halifax? And Liscomb was a lot closer to Louisburg than Halifax. If none of this is true, how did the mystery items come to be among the rest of the sodden reminders of a maiden voyage horribly concluded amid the unheard cries of a doomed crew? Only the sea can know.

For the record: *Halifax No 19* was claimed to be the most modern lightship in the world at the time of her construction. Built throughout of mild steel, her designers had given her a clipper bow and an elliptical stern. Much care had been lavished on her capacity to survive and the watertight bulkheads were so arranged that the ship would remain afloat even if two compartments were completely flooded. Once fitted out she would have carried a revolving lantern crafted by Barbier of Paris, perched upon a heavy steel tower. Access to the light was to have been by internal stairway. The main foghorn on the spar deck just forward of the lantern tower was to be driven by air pressure tanks in the forward hold.

Deck equipment included a small steam winch for working the boats and a much heavier winch for veering out and drawing in the massive mooring chains. Part of the fully electric internal lighting system was a steam turbo generating set in the engine room and, also steam-powered, a central heating system was included as were fresh water washing facilities. The fresh water capacity of 7000 gallons was to be augmented by rainwater barrels on deck. Another back-up system was the evaporating and distilling plant capable of changing 2000 gallons of seawater to fresh every 24 hours.

Two Scottish coal-fired boilers supplied steam at a working pressure of 110 lbs per square inch. Motive power consisted of one set of fore and aft compound engines driving a right-hand, four-bladed propeller. The complement of independent auxiliaries included air circulation, feed, bilge and sanitary pumps. Her radio telephone equipment was ahead of its time. The first British lightship to be so equipped was the vessel on the South Goodwin station in 1922.

The boats of *Halifax No 19* were one 23-foot lifeboat on the port side and, among the mass of equipment waiting at Halifax, one 31-foot motor launch to be situated on the starboard side.

LIGHT BITES

The year 1883 had just nine hours to run when the *Abertay* Lightship was approached from upriver by a group of rowing boats and a steam launch. No-one in the boats was rowing and no smoke issued from the funnel of the launch yet on they came, the occupants gesticulating wildly. The vessels, now seen to be linked by lines, appeared to be in the grip of some unseen force. The mystery was solved when the flotilla came to a halt over the Gaa Sands and a huge whale breached among them. The chasing pack had twice harpooned the animal but a line had parted, leaving just one holding the hoped-for prize. The launch, the *Storm King*, proceeded to the lightship and borrowed some hand-held lanterns to continue the hunt in the gathering darkness. It was still dark when she and the rowing boats returned with the lanterns on New Year's Day. Gratefully accepting the hot breakfast offered by the Master of the lightship, plus a measure of Hogmanay spirit, the men gradually thawed out. They had an extraordinary tale to tell of their night on the North Sea. Only with great difficulty had the *Storm King* relocated the boats which were being towed rapidly north-east. The whale took them on an erratic course all the way to Scurdyness lighthouse off Montrose, turned south and dragged them past the Bell Rock towards the Forth estuary then back to the Bell Rock before the last line broke. The whale had first been harpooned near Broughty Ferry so the distance it had pulled them could not have been far short of 50 miles. The hunters had been lucky that the distressed creature, needing to breathe often, had not gone deep. The value of this '60-foot hunchback' was estimated at £130.

LIGHT BITES

On January 25th, 1988, the 140-ton *LV 78* (*Calshot Spit*) was lifted out of the water at the Ocean Village Marina, Southampton and placed into a specially dug pit on the quay where she has been on display ever since, two metres of the vessel permanently underground. Two cranes carried out the lift. One of these was transported in sections from Stockton-on-Tees on 24 articulated trucks. When fully assembled its counterbalance weight was 175 tons and it had seven axles.

LV 78 (*Calshot Spit*) in mid-air on her way to a permanent display site. Photograph courtesy of Paul Carter.

LV 78 (*Calshot Spit*) on the quay at Ocean Village, Southampton.

The Newarp Lightship Station

*N*ot every lightship station was the result of a cold, calculated decision on where best to locate it. Sometimes a station was introduced quite literally by accident. This was the case when the British steamer *Scotland* sank in the approaches to New York Harbour.

A relief lightship, *LS 20*, was placed near the wreck on April 15th, 1868 with the words *Wreck of the Scotland* painted in white on her sides. It was a temporary task which was eventually to become permanent. Even after the wreck had been dragged into deeper water and was no longer a menace to shipping, shipowners, including Cunard Line Steamers, campaigned to keep the lightship in place.

Their petition was persuasive, claiming that the lightship was 'of such great benefit to the masters and pilots of the ships entering and leaving the port that its removal would prove a serious injury to navigation'. But Admiral W.B. Shubrick, Chief of the Lighthouse Bureau in Washington DC had previously issued on November 2nd 1870, Notice to Mariners No. 112 to the effect that the *Wreck of the Scotland* Lightship would be removed on December 5th.

When *LS 20* was indeed removed and laid up in Mulford Basin, Staten Island, it looked as though the shipowners' battle against the Bureau had been in vain. But they were like terriers with a bone and continued to petition for restoration of the light vessel station. Finally they got their way and in September of 1874, *LS 23* was placed at the site.

The shipowners did have a point. Traffic into the port of New York was exceptionally heavy. In 1878 shipping movements between the *Wreck of the Scotland* Lightship and the *Sandy Hook* Lightship nearby consisted of: 3346 steamships; 5283 barquentines; 1517 brigantines; 6885 schooners and 1073 other vessels. The station, which was eventually moved half a mile from its original position and renamed simply *Scotland*, became an indispensable link in the chain of lights leading to the harbour of New York.

LS 20, often used as a relief lightship by the US Lighthouse Authorities, was moored on April 10th, 1886 to mark the wreck of the *Oregon* 13 miles off Long Island. The masts of the ill-fated ship can be seen to the left of this engraving. *Harper's Weekly*, April 24th, 1886.

In common with most other lightship stations in United States waters, it was suspended during the Second World War. Not every light vessel station was returned to duty on the cessation of hostilities but the *Scotland* was one of those selected for reactivation. It was retained in operation until 1966 when it was replaced by a buoy.

If it took an accident to establish the *Wreck of the Scotland*, what led to the introduction of *The Newarp* Lightship station off the east coast of England was a catastrophe – one of the major shipping tragedies of the 18th century. In view of what occurred, it seems almost cruel to identify any beneficial consequence. Yet not only did the event lead to the anchoring of the first lightship at The Newarp in 1791 but it was pivotal to the advance of lightships as a concept.

Although Trinity House already had three lightship stations under its jurisdiction – the only ones in the world at that time – some members of the organisation remained unconvinced about the ability of the ships to remain in position and an application for a patent to moor a lightship in the general area of The Newarp had already been refused in 1739. There was good reason for their doubts. One vessel, at the Owers station off Portsmouth, had been blown so far from its mooring that it ended up in another country – France.

What happened in the storm off the Norfolk coast on Friday, October 30th, 1789 helped to dispel those doubts and paved the way for an explosion in the number of lightships and their spread throughout most of the maritime world. Trinity House ordered more than 100 in rather less than a century from that date, notwithstanding a period of relative stagnation during the long years of the Napoleonic War which ended in 1815.

The following extract from a letter published in *The Times* four days after the 1789 storm paints a graphic picture of the risks of going to sea in the days of sail:

A large fleet of ships was lying in the Roads of Yarmouth, several of which, being driven from their anchors and running foul of one another, great confusion took place.

Some foundered, many lost their masts; while others were obliged to slip or cut their cables and run to the southward which, luckily for them on account of the quarter from which the wind blew, they could without much danger so that only two were forced onto the shore to the south of the harbour.

The case however, of those vessels caught by the storm to the northward of the Cockle Sand was infinitely more distressing and fatal.

Such of them as were at anchor waiting for the light to enter the Roads were almost all forced to quit their anchors by the violence of the wind or by other ships coming athwart them; some sank instantly upon collision; others perished the moment they were driven on the land; some, having beaten over the Cockle Sand, either went down in deep water or fell upon the Barber.*

In the days before the telegraph cable was laid linking the United States with Europe, the *Sandy Hook* Lightship (*LS 16*) near New York harbour could spark frantic activity in the Stock Market there. Passing ships would often throw a pile of newspapers aboard the ship and from there a summary of the main events would be telegraphed to the shore. The ships which had parted with the papers at *Sandy Hook* often tied up in harbour to find Wall Street already convulsed by news from the lightship. The *Sandy Hook* lightship station was renamed *Ambrose* early in the 20th century. It was America's first 'open sea' lightship station. *Harper's Weekly*, September 27th, 1879.

Nothing can be conceived more dreadful than the morning aspect from this place. The walls of the town were lined with persons of all ages, sexes and conditions.

Distress and anxiety were printed upon the countenance of every one you accosted. On account of the fishing season being at its height, there was not a poor person who had not a father or a husband or a son for whose fate they were not all alarm; nor a rich person who had not some property either in ships or in boats and nets for which he felt himself interested.

Everyone you met had his own tale of woe; of his seeing a vessel going down in this quarter or in that.

But indeed there was no occasion to listen to what had taken place, there was enough of distressing prospect to be seen even for him who latest left his downy bed.

Ships from the northward were every moment coming in, some with every sail split, hanging like so many pennants; others came with one mast only standing; others with nothing but a small piece of canvas fastened to the remaining stumps of their masts; others with all their boats and anchors washed away; others in a perfectly unmanageable state, driving through the Roads at the mercy of the waves and at last sinking in sight of hundreds of spectators.

In short, our shores are literally covered with pieces of wreck and dead bodies are hourly washing up.

Included in Lloyd's list of ships damaged and sunk was the Sudis of Whitby, one of a number of vessels whose entire crews were lost. The final count showed 23 ships sunk, 20 driven on shore. The number of fatalities was in the region of 600.

Part of the blame for the disaster was placed on the absence of good navigation lights on and about the coastline. So *The Newarp* Lightship station came into being eight miles offshore and one mile from the north end of the Newarp Bank. Improvements were also made to the onshore lights. Many lightships served at The Newarp over a spell of nearly 200 years, dishing out their unique brand of preventive medicine at no little cost to themselves.

During the Second World War alone, two ships and one light float were sunk at The Newarp, all unmanned. The unmanned ships were introduced after several attacks took place on manned Norfolk lightships during March, 1940. German bombers – earning for themselves the nickname 'The Murder Planes' – were able to launch attacks on the lightships by employing a new tactic of flying in at dusk or dawn showing all their lights in an attempt to simulate the practice of British bomber pilots returning to base.

Another *Newarp* ship was sunk after being rammed by a freighter on August 15th, 1967.

*The Barber is a sandbank, located about two miles east of the lifeboat shed at Caister. In the days of sail it was an extreme hazard to shipping. Nowadays, it is called the Caister Shoal.

LS 50
(Columbia River)

*T*he Pacific coast of north-western America is a wild and lonely place for a man to spend his working life. But many a seaman did just that aboard the light-ships that served there and a perceptive insight into life aboard the *Columbia River* Lightship in this environment, marking the bar at the river mouth, is contained in a letter written by one master to the Lighthouse Literary Mission in Belfast. This was a charitable organisation which sent books, magazines and other reading material to lighthouse keepers and lightship crewmen worldwide.

The letter is undated but was certainly written at some time prior to 1936. The skipper writes:

This vessel is a fine, steel-built vessel of 487 tons, with a crew of fourteen men, anchored off the Columbia River sea coast of Oregon; very dangerous place, having the whole Pacific Ocean down on us sometimes; always danger of breaking adrift and going on the bar.

However, we have a good vessel and plenty of steam power. It is in the winter we have our most worriesome times. South-east gales are always accompanied by dense fog and if the vessel should happen to drift without us knowing, we are likely to lead some other ship on to destruction. For three months of the year — December, January and February — all hands are on board, no liberty granted and you may be sure we are glad when the winter is over. Sometimes we are lucky enough to be of service to unfortunate shipwrecked sailors having been wrecked on the coast and getting off in small boats. They always try to make for the lightship.

We are the proud possessors of commendations from the Lighthouse Bureau at Washington for prompt action in picking up boats with shipwrecked crews. One instance: a steamer had been wrecked about forty miles down the coast in a heavy S.E. gale; ten men of the crew were lucky enough to get off in a small boat; the only chance was to get picked up by the lightship.

They came drifting down on us in a dark, stormy night. We were able to pick them up by being always well-prepared and keeping a good look-out. Had they drifted by us nothing could have saved them, for they were nearly all in.

I do not know what keeps one on in this kind of work but we are still here year by year. Close by this vessel are several old sea captains and bar pilots buried, they having spent their life in piloting vessels safely over the bar, and when dying requested their ashes to be buried outside the bar.

Their ashes have been sunk in hollow cement blocks. Poor fellows, I knew them when they were alive. Big-hearted and brave men, always around in their pilot boat in thick weather and thin.

Even now, in gloomy and threatening weather, some of my crew contend they see the pilot's light dancing among the waves – a sure sign of a coming storm.

Although not specifically identified in the letter, the ship seems certain to have been *LS 88*, the longest-lived of all the lightships which served at the location. Her last year there was 1939.

LS 88 was taken out of commission in 1959 after a career lasting half a century. When last heard of, having been converted into a two-masted square-rigged brigantine called the *Belle Blonde II*, she was plying the St Lawrence River, Canada as a charter vessel. The writer of the letter referred to the constant fear of the ship parting her mooring. He had particular reason for this concern because it had happened before, with extraordinary consequences.

The Columbia River Lightship station, the first on America's west coast, was established in 1892. Its first ship was *LS 50* which had a wooden hull enveloping frames of steel. She carried a distillation plant to make drinking water from seawater.

On November 29th, 1899, a gale with wind speeds of 74 mph raised very heavy seas. Sometime during the afternoon the cable snapped 270 feet from the hawse-pipe. Original plans for the ship included giving her a steam engine but this had not been carried through. At that moment how the crew must have wished it had! Having managed to retrieve the remains of the anchor cable, the men could only hoist their sails in an effort to hold the ship offshore until the next morning in the hope that the storm would by that time have spent some of its fury.

Next day *LS 50* set a course for the river mouth, although breakers were running dangerously high over the bar. The tug *Wallula* and the tender *Manzanita* were sent to assist. Both ships managed to get lines aboard the lightship but both parted, one of them fouling the propeller of the *Manzanita*. Another tug, the *Escort*, did secure a line to *LS 50* and began towing her across the bar. Halfway over, the line parted and the lightship was now adrift in the breakers off McKenzie Head.

According to the local lighthouse district report:

In order to save the crew and if possible the vessel, extreme measures were necessary and it was decided to beach the vessel.

To the north of McKenzie Head was a rock-bound coast lashed by angry seas. A short distance below was Fort Canby and the rocks of the southern end of Cape Disappointment.

Between these two promontories lies a sandy beach. To put the ship on this beach meant the probable saving of men and ship, while to strike the rocks on either side meant death to the crew and destruction to the vessel.

It was a great tribute to the crew that *LS 50* grounded at the right spot at 6.30 pm. The master had used his sails to swing the ship into the surf, pointing the high prow into the breakers. The men were brought ashore by breeches buoy by the crew of the Cape Disappointment Life Saving Service station. People from the local Army base and civilians also took part in the rescue.

Once conditions had calmed down, moveable items were taken from the ship and bids were sought from contractors to have her refloated. There were several attempts made to have the ship removed to seaward, all of which failed. It was left to a furniture removal company from Portland, Oregon to put in a bid of $17,000 to move the lightship across land to a point where she could be relaunched into the sheltered waters of Bakers Bay.

After many delays and false starts, *LS 50* found herself being jacked onto a cradle and settled onto a temporary railway which ran for 700 yards along the sand spit and through woods to the bay. The lightship had been stranded for 16 months. By the time the contractor had been paid and repairs carried out, expenses had mounted to over half the cost of building the ship. *LS 50* was placed back on station on August 18th, 1901 and served there until 1909.

LS 50 being pulled along a specially-built railway track to a point in Bakers Bay where she was relaunched. With permission from the U. S. Lighthouse Society.

Charles Acey, who spent almost 20 years as a crewman on the *Spurn* Lightship, was a keen ornithologist and kept a log of the different species of birds he saw from the ship. Among the exotic types was a long-eared owl which was being mobbed by seagulls. But perhaps the most unusual happening involved the common starling which descended on the ship's lantern in such numbers during a heavy fog that the light became almost invisible.

It was commonplace aboard light vessels to pass the long weary hours by practising various arts and crafts. The men made toys, furniture, rope slippers etc. The thing to do aboard Nantucket ships was basket-making. A few of these baskets survive today, some of which are now antiques. They have become collectors' items but no-one could have anticipated the price achieved at Sotheby's New York auction of January, 1994 for a nest of six baskets made by crewman Davis Hall – $118,000 including commissions. That's about $20,000 (£13,000) per basket.

Swing-handle basket by crewman Davis Hall (1828-1905).
Photograph: Nantucket Historical Association.

LV 38
(Gull, Brake)

On the withdrawal of *LV 29* from the Gull station in the north-western corner of the Goodwin Sands in early March, 1929, a newer ship took over. This was *LV 38*, built by Charles Hill at Bristol in 1860. Her baptism at the Gull was destined to be depressingly complete.

As an anti-cyclone settled over southern Britain that month a fine, settled spell of weather ensued with inland counties of England basking in almost uninterrupted sunshine. But high pressure could also mean fog and the Channel coast was plagued by it.

The transferred crew of *LV 29* were soon into their stride, getting plenty of practice at blowing the triple reed foghorn on their new ship. On the night of March 18th, the fog was very dense and their signal was in constant operation. Foghorns and whistles were sounding all around from other ships under way. It was a worrying time for those crewmen on watch as the dark hours dragged by. Midnight passed but the danger remained, with no slackening in the volume of shipping passing close by.

At 4 am the lights of a large steamer suddenly appeared. There was no time to react. With a sickening crash, the bows of the ship bit deep into the port side of *LV 38*, almost amidships. The lightship was mortally wounded, cut right down below the waterline. Those crewmen who had been asleep below fell out of their hammocks and rushed topside. The ship was sinking fast. Just one lifeboat remained intact but even as they struggled to launch it, the ship disappeared under them.

The steamer, the 7834-ton Ellerman Line *SS City of York*, bound for London, had anchored and was now sounding SOS on its siren. A boat launched from the *City of York* managed to locate the crew as they trod water. All were taken safely aboard, suffering from exposure. The ship's doctor had them wrapped in hot blankets and put to bed. But the Master of the *Gull*, Captain W. Williams, was missing. His cabin had been close to the point of impact and it was feared he had gone down with the lightship.

LV 38 on the Brake Station. The two black cones, point to point at the masthead, make a distinctive daymark. At night her lantern delivered a single flash of red light every 20 seconds.

At Deal, just a few miles away, it was soon realised that something was amiss. Harry Meakins set off in his small clinker-built boat *Lady Beatty*, which provided a regular service for some of the Goodwin Sands light vessels. Another boat, the *Terrier*, also made its way to the scene and both were later joined by the Ramsgate lifeboat.

Harry Meakins found the spot where the *Gull* Lightship had sunk in 7½ fathoms, her double-cone daymark still above water. Visibility was down to one to two yards. Meakins recalled:

> *'It was terribly risky work, moving about as we did amid lots of wreckage in a fog so thick, with innumerable steamers groping all around us with their hooters and foghorns sounding. We could hear one big ship blowing all her foghorns at once so close that we went to her and found it was the City of York.*
>
> *The captain informed us he had six men on board whom he had picked out of the water but that the Master of the lightship was still unaccounted for. We went back to the spot and made a further search but without result and we reluctantly gave up.'*

But this effort was not to mark the end of their work. The boats returned to port about 7 a.m. and the *City of York* made her way to London where the lightship crew got ashore on the evening of March 19th.

Back at Deal, Meakins found he had a new task to perform. A message from Trinity House awaited him, asking if his boat could act as a replacement for the lightship until a tender vessel arrived. Meakins got hold of an old fog signal apparatus, flares and a large bell. With this gear aboard, the *Lady Beatty* again put to sea, with crew members Charlie and Dave Pritchard, Edward Griggs, Dick Brown and Tommy Baker. On arrival at the wreck site, they started sounding the signal at the required rate for the Gull station – two blasts every two minutes.

Dick Brown went so far as to clamber onto the ship's daymark to which he attached a green wreck flag and proceeded to spend hours there sounding the bell. The men carried on this work without relief until 5p.m. They had come close to suffering the same fate as the lightship, several vessels shearing away from them at the last moment.

Note: The crew of the *Lady Beatty* may have made a tiny piece of lightship history. No records studied to date refer to such a small vessel acting as a replacement lightship, although the *Hough's Neck* Lightship was claimed to be the world's smallest during its single-summer spell moored over a sand bar near Hough's Neck, Massachusetts in 1909. The 'lightship' was a 19-foot dory anchored at the bar by Joseph C. Riley, captain of the local steamer.

Riley had it painted red with a white band amidships. The dory had two masts, each carrying a petrol can. Two red lanterns hung from her rigging. She carried the name *Hough's Neck* Lightship with the number 15 painted below because the fare on the steamer was 15 cents. The vessel was never officially recognised as a lightship.

When divers were able to explore the wreck of *LV 38*, they found the body of Captain Williams, who had been trapped in his cabin. It was not long before a new chapter opened in the career of the ship. She was raised four months after the collision and taken to the River Tyne for a complete refit before being returned to the Goodwin Sands in 1930, this time marking the Brake Sand.

This was a brand-new light vessel station for the Goodwin Sands. The ship was still on the Gull stream but on the west side instead of the east at a point to seaward of the Brake Patch. It displayed a red light. On its old anchorage now bobbed the North-West Goodwins buoy, showing a newly-installed light which delivered a white flash four times every 15 seconds. The Brake station was intended as a short-term arrangement but it worked so well that Trinity House made it permanent.

With the onset of war in 1939, the ship was manned on a part-time basis, the light being lit only when a convoy was due. The start of 1940 introduced a period of terrible weather. On January 16th, a blizzard was blowing from the north-east. Many ships were anchored in The Downs, an area between the Goodwins and the shore, as they awaited clearance from contraband control at Ramsgate.

One of these ships, the Italian steamer *Ernani* began to drag her anchor. In bad visibility, at about 7 pm the 6600-ton ship struck *LV 38* in the bow area, holing her close to the waterline. Master of the lightship, Mr. J. Beet, was faced with a difficult decision. If the stowage locker for the ship's chain became flooded, the lightship must sink. But if the crew left the ship in one of the boats, they faced great danger. Beet decided they must abandon ship.

LV 38 in a decayed state at
Grays, Essex. The old lightship
has been in its present location
since 1947, when it was
purchased by Thurrock Yacht
Club for use as a clubhouse.
Thurrock Museum postcard.

With great difficulty a lifeboat was lowered but it was apparent from the start that
it was going to be too risky to try to board the *Ernani*. The crew were forced to row
around in the snowstorm, looking for another vessel which might be able to take
them aboard. Spray froze on the men, who had to bale furiously to keep their small
craft afloat. Just when it looked as though they could not survive, the control zone
guardship *HMS Holdfast* appeared and the light vessel crew managed to clamber
aboard. On the morning of the 17th, the Ramsgate lifeboat took off the crew and
landed them on a shore which was two feet deep in snow in places. Beet and two of
his men had to be treated for exposure and frostbite.

LV 38 had remained afloat and some of her crew were returned to the ship at 1 pm
that same day and began to cover the hole in the side. It was a task which took some
days and the lightship was then towed to Harwich, stern first, for a complete repair.

Although *LV 38* served again briefly at the Mouse station in the Thames
approaches, she spent most of the war laid up at Great Yarmouth. The *Brake*
Lightship station was discontinued after the war, being replaced by a buoy. Although
the Trinity House Approving Lights Committee recommended a resumption of the
lightship station at their meeting on October 13th, 1953, this course of action was
not followed.

LV 38 served as a clubhouse for the Thurrock Yacht Club for a time, despite her reputation for being haunted, presumably by the spirit of her dead Master, Captain Williams. At the time of writing, the wood-built vessel is in dire straits, rotting on the Thames mud at Grays, Essex. She is the sole surviving lightship of her type, the lantern still in place.

Another former Trinity House light vessel, *LV 50*, has served as the clubhouse for the Royal Northumberland Yacht Club at Blyth Harbour since 1952 at which time she was being held in reserve on the Isle of Wight. Among her former stations was the Calshot Spit off Southampton. She was the last lightship to be built entirely of wood – mostly teak which in places was eight inches thick. She is periodically inspected and during one such survey, an attempt to drill into the stem post ended when the metal bit broke.

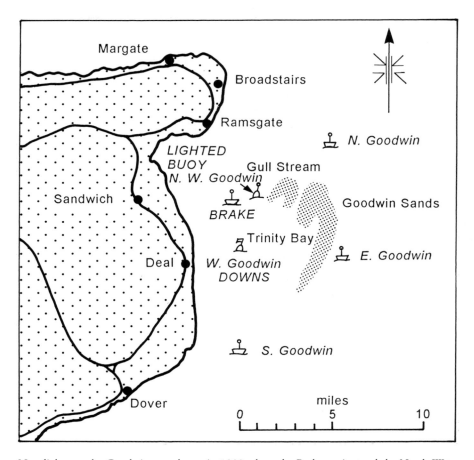

New lights on the Goodwins are shown in 1930 where the Brake station and the North-West Goodwin lighted buoy straddle the area of the Gull stream.

LIGHT BITES

Light vessel Master William Palmer recalled the time aboard the *Lynn Well* Lightship in The Wash, off England's east coast, when a small seal appeared alongside crying like a baby. The crewman on watch at first thought there was someone in the water. When the men realised what it was they managed to get it on board. The seal seemed to have lost its mother so they fed it on Nestlé's milk and it thrived. 'It was with us for a long time,' said Mr Palmer. 'We would open the gangway door and he flapped through it into the water and went for a swim. Back he would come and almost ask us to take him aboard again. We lifted him out of the water in a hoop net and he would flap about the deck, following us around. I don't know if it was Spring in the air and he had found a mate but one day he went for his usual dip and cleared off. We never saw him again.' BBC Radio Children's Hour, June 15th, 1942.

In 1929 the crew of the *Spurn* Lightship asked the Humber Conservancy Board for more money when the fog signal was in operation. This was reluctantly agreed but when the crew of the *Bull* Lightship asked for the same treatment since they were, as they put it 'enduring the same fog' the Board replied with unconscious humour, 'We cannot see our way to paying.' In 1932 the Mission To Seamen in London offered to provide a wireless set for the entertainment of the men on the *Bull* Lightship. The Board refused to allow the donation.

The gimbals used in every light vessel to keep its light level with the horizon were the product of the suspension principle invented in the 16th century by Italian scientist Girolamo Cardan. The object to be kept in a vertical position, e.g. an oil lamp, was held on two pivots at opposite ends of the diameter of a ring which was itself pivoted at two points at opposite ends of a diameter at right angles to the first, to a fixed support.

Built in 1950 at Curtis Bay, Maryland, *LS 612* spent most of her service on the San Francisco (Bar) station. Part of the main hold was converted into a gymnasium for the crew of 12. Other pastimes included fishing from the ship's motor launch, taking correspondence courses run by the Armed Forces Institute and operating a radio 'ham' station on board.

Reading Lights

The network of navigation lights approaching rivers or ports, or grouped in a defensive shield to the seaward side of hazards like a string of sandbanks were life-saving devices, to put it simply. Almost always the lightships were the outermost of these markers, the first indicators of their own position to vessels nearing the coastline. Where there had to be many of these packed into a small area, it could prove difficult to sort out which was which and great care went into deciding the characteristic for each light. A mistake made here by a navigator could have disastrous consequences.

When Captain O.P. Kaspersen left the Norwegian port of Brevik on Saturday, March 18th, 1899 with a cargo of ice, he was taking the first steps along a route to ignominy trod by many an experienced seaman before him. Kaspersen and his crew of seven were bound for the English Channel port of Newhaven, near Brighton.

The Norwegian was proud of his ship. He had bought the Tonsberg-registered *Iduna* less than a year before. A graceful, three-masted schooner she was, all 340 tons of her, sound as a bell. Norway's relative lack of coal and iron deposits kept the sails of the nation filling well beyond the time when most other European countries had turned to steamships. As late as 1914, 275 Norwegian sailing vessels were still engaged in trade.

The North Sea was in sullen mood with strong to gale-force westerly winds and it took the *Iduna* five days of hard sailing to close the east coast of England off Norfolk. Here, the waves became even heavier.

It was still dark early on Thursday morning when the *Smith's Knoll* Lightship was sighted. Kaspersen set his course accordingly. The *Iduna* was now doomed. For the light vessel actually seen by Kaspersen was the *Leman & Ower* 10 miles north of the Smith's Knoll. Before the skipper realised his mistake the *Iduna* had crossed a sandbar and piled up on the rocks beyond. With their ship rapidly sinking under them the crew launched a boat and rowed in seething, churning white water to the nearby lightship. Drenched and chilled to the bone, they were helped aboard.

They remained for two days on the *Leman & Ower* until on Saturday morning, Captain Meyre of the steamer *Gironde* interrupted his trip from Rotterdam to Aberdeen to take them off. Once landed in the Granite City the crew were settled into the Sailors' Institute in James Street where their wants were attended to by the Superintendent, Mr Coull.

At an initial inquiry into the loss of the *Iduna* on behalf of the Norwegian Board of Trade, the Norwegian Consul representative, Mr Cook, took evidence from the crew in his office at 62 Marischal Street, Aberdeen. Captain Kaspersen stated that the lights of the two light vessels were similar and this had led him into the error that cost him his ship and his crew all their worldly possessions. The captain was mistaken.

The *Leman & Ower* Lightship station was established in 1849 as one of several marking the banks off Norfolk. The *Smith's Knoll* was another of these Yarmouth-based lightships. However, according to the Trinity House data for the period, the light characteristics were quite different.

The *Leman & Ower* carried two lights, one fixed white aft at 27 feet above the waterline, the other a revolving light for'ard, hoisted every night to a height of 38 feet above the waterline. The *Smith's Knoll* displayed one group flashing light, alternately white and red. If Kaspersen was sure he'd raised the *Smith's Knoll*, he should have seen some red.

The reason for his mistake may be contained in a telling phrase used by the mate of the old *South Shoal* Lightship off Massachusetts as he studied through his telescope the errant antics of a sailing ship floundering around trying to find the lightship.

'These captains feel so sure of their course,' he said, 'that they always expect to raise us dead ahead.'

Maybe Kaspersen expected to raise the *Smith's Knoll* and persuaded himself he had done so. Like today's car driver, certain he is better than he really is, the skipper could have over-valued his own capabilities. This is not to diminish the difficulties faced by the captain entering a region like the Norfolk sandbanks with its spread of different lights. It is worth examining the two lightships involved in the Kaspersen case.

One disadvantage of a lightship like the *Leman & Ower*, with lights on more than one mast, concerned the appearance of the lights when the masts were in line. Clearly their aspect would differ from the normal pattern. Seen fleetingly in poor visibility, confusion might ensue.

When Robert Stevenson moored his lightship near the Bell Rock in 1806 (see *LV Pharos*) he included in his Notice to Mariners not just the information that his vessel carried three lights, one on each mast, the centre being the highest. He was at pains to point out that with the masts in line the lights would appear as one on top of the other.

The *Smith's Knoll* light, with its red element, may also have presented a problem. Red light projects just 40% the distance of white and despite the availability of magnifying devices to improve the range of coloured lights, this part of the ship's night-time 'identity tag' may not have been visible on every occasion. (Green light was occasionally used on lightships. The colour was able to penetrate just one quarter the distance of white.)

Leaving aside the particulars of the *Iduna* loss, it must be pertinent to note that inquiries into such accidents always suffered from the same weakness. Only those on the ship knew what they saw or did not see through driving rain, or snow, or spray, or mist, or uncertain light. Many a career at sea has been ruined by definitive judgements made in the calm, warm atmosphere of an office on the shore. That many of them were wide of the mark is a racing certainty.

Kaspersen's expensive entanglement with English lightships came at a time when there were no such vessels in the waters of his own country, yet Norwegians had already managed a brief flirtation with lightships – their first lasted just 96 days. The catalyst for its eventual introduction came in 1839 when a survey of navigation equipment aboard 200 trading vessels revealed a total of five sextants and two chronometers between the lot.

Stunned by the survey results, the maritime authorities hustled in one year later the first-ever qualifying examination for skippers and mates followed in 1844 by the first school of navigation based at Kristiana. This facility was desperately needed for much of the coastline remained to be charted in detail and the provision of light-houses, light buoys and other navigation aids would not get under way until the 1850s.

Undoubtedly encouraged by their new formal training, the Norwegians embarked upon what is still today described as 'the golden age' for seaborne trade. This progress was given a further shot in the arm by the repeal of the British Navigation Act in 1849 which threw open the trade of the entire British Empire to non-British carriers. Norwegians seized the opportunities better than anyone else, including the freighting of supplies to the Crimea for the war raging there. During the two decades commencing 1860, their merchant fleet was the third largest in the world. However, as the fleet grew, concern increased about finding ways to make the country's extensive coastline safer for this flourishing commerce. Discussion centred on what was later to become known as the 1100-nautical mile 'express route' from Bergen via Trondheim to the Arctic circle settlement of Kirkenes.

During 1851 there was much agonising over one area on the route where just five metres of water covered a reef – the Lepsøyrev – about nine nautical miles north of Alesund. A buoy did exist, as yet unlit, and it was felt some form of beacon was needed after dusk. A lightship was finally agreed upon and the sloop Enigheden, a trader of 27 cubic metres of cargo space, was purchased and converted at Alesund for lightship duty. The mast and sails were removed and a new mast fitted with a block and tackle arrangement for hoisting and lowering the lantern. The lantern itself was made of iron and had a pane of glass on each of its six sides. It housed an oil lamp with a reflector. The ship was given new, heavier chain, a bigger anchor and a new set of sails to enable her to get to and from her mooring near Haram village in an area dotted with islands. On December 5th, 1856, the fixed white light of the *Lepsøyrev* Lightship first shone out. Positioned 7.5 metres above the waterline the light did not carry far – four nautical miles in good conditions. No one could have guessed that the ship would be short on good luck too.

One of the crew died after a month on duty and before he could be replaced the ship was caught in a violent storm from the north-west on March 11th, 1857 and driven aground 400 metres off station. It took such a battering that it had to be condemned. The wreck was more or less given away at auction for 13.5 spd (Spesiedaler), the coinage which would be superseded by the krone in 1873. In British currency the sale was worth about £2.14s., which certainly reflected the stipulation that the purchaser had to remove the wreck.

Clearly a bigger, stronger vessel was required to withstand winter storms. During May, Norway's Director of Lighthouses visited Denmark to acquaint himself better with the construction and deployment of light vessels. The Danes had considerable experience in this field, their first lightship having been laid in 1829. Armed with his new-found expertise, the Director returned home and another lightship was commissioned. Completed in December, 1857 it was 12 metres long and constructed of oak, as were Danish lightships, had a distinctive keel and was copper-sheathed below the waterline. The vessel was painted red and carried the lettering *Lepsøyrev Fyrskip* in white letters along each flank. Like its predecessor the light delivered a fixed white beam, first shown on January 8th, 1858. The ship had no fog signal but when this was introduced in 1860 it was sounded every 15 minutes. The anchorage proved troublesome and caused much wear and friction on the mooring so after two years the ship had to be moved to another location nearby.

In 1866 an even bigger lightship was built at Hommelvik on Trondheim Fjord. 16 metres long and four metres in the beam, it was moored beside the *Lepsøyrev* until that ship was removed and placed in reserve at Alesund during August, 1867. In 1872 the station's fog signal was altered to sound once every five minutes. Crew of the new *Lepsøyrev* consisted of a lightsman, three seamen and a cabin boy except during summer when just two men worked the ship.

The light vessel proved expensive to run and maintain compared to light stations on land. It had to be slipped for instance, to have its hull greased. Since the lifespan of the ship was estimated at between eight and ten years, it was decided to build a light on land to replace it. In 1879 the lighthouse was completed and the lightship was removed for the last time from its position 1500 metres to the south-west of the land light. It was sold at auction for 1001 krone, with the reserve ship also sold, for 200 krone. The lightships had won the affection of the skippers and seamen using the route but operating them had posed unusual problems. The coastline was precipitous, very deep water often found just a few metres from the shoreline. Especially long mooring chains were required. Also, it was extremely difficult to find good holding ground for anchors. The bottom of the hundreds of frigid fjords thrusting deep into the land was almost universally of rock and divers hunting for a suitable site frequently found huge boulders littering the sea floor. A lightship could easily be driven off that kind of ground with potentially fatal consequences. Another drawback was the extreme strength of some of the tides racing through narrow sounds and fjords. The notorious Saltstraum at Bodo near the Lofoten Islands for instance, can reach speeds of 16 knots on both ebb and flood. It was scarcely surprising that Norway produced just one more light vessel station. This came to be sited in the fjord leading to the principal port of Kristiana (renamed Oslo in 1925).

In 1872 the dangerous Ildjerns flu (rock) was marked by a black and white buoy. By 1914 this had been replaced by a lighted buoy but the seamen's union in Kristiana remained dissatisfied and a committee was formed to consider three alternatives for improving safety at the location. They considered 1): making no change and sticking with the lighted buoy; 2): some form of fixed structure; 3): dynamiting the rock. In the end none of these options found favour and the committee decided to opt for a lightship. In 1919, a flat-bottomed, iron-built vessel, ballasted with reinforced concrete, was placed at the rock 1.3 nautical miles south-west of Nesoddtangen. The ship was equipped with an acetylene gas light of the 4th order delivering 1830 candlepower, carried nine metres above the sea. It gave one flash every five seconds, visible up to 10.5 nautical miles away. Its foghorn was driven by a small petrol engine.

In 1929 the ship was rammed and sunk. A year later a new lightship – built of wood in a reversal of the customary trend – took its place. Its light, perched on a short mast protruding from the forward section of the white-painted deckhouse, looked like an afterthought. The ship was painted red, divided by a white stripe halfway between the deck and the sea. The name *Ildjernsflu* was borne above the stripe. The flag of the lighthouse service fluttered from the stern.

The last light vessel to serve in Norwegian waters, the *Ildjernsflu Fyrskip* was upgraded from time to time. The fog signal was improved in 1940 with the introduction of a siren but the next major move in 1968 meant the end of the lightship which, by that time, had deteriorated to such an extent that it was decommissioned. A circular concrete structure was towed out to take its place and fixed to the bottom in about six metres of water. It had an electrically-driven light and a nautophone fog signal, both operated via a cable from the shore.

The Abertay Lightship (1877–1939)

*T*he *Abertay* Lightship station was born out of a bitter dispute. Throughout the middle years of the 19th century, an argument simmered between the Fraternity of Masters and Seamen in Dundee, also known as Trinity House after their office at Yeaman Shore, and the Dundee Harbour Trust over whether or not to have a light vessel to augment the navigation aids in the River Tay.

The Fraternity had managed the navigation of the river for nearly 300 years. On February 24th, 1687 the Privy Council granted them a warrant to erect lights and beacons in the Tay and the right to charge for the lights a sum of 12 pennies Scots for each ton of cargo in outgoing and incoming British vessels. For overseas traders the sum was two shillings Scots per ton. It was a major step forward for the Fraternity. The light dues applied to ships entering and leaving the harbours on both banks and the fees helped pay the pensions of the widows of members. In 1867 there were 113 widows and seven children eligible for pension payments. This was a heavy drain on the body's resources and spoke volumes for the perils of going to sea in those far-off times.

Their extreme reluctance to concede the need for a lightship probably had much to do with the expense of providing and maintaining it. As early as 1847 the Trust were annoying their rivals with suggested new navigation aids in the Tay, including a 'red lightship' three quarters of a mile west of Tentsmuir Point. The Fraternity were incensed and claimed that such a floating light would only encourage 'foolhardy navigators' to attempt crossing the Tay bar at night instead of waiting for daylight.

They also produced a letter from the Bell Rock Lighthouse engineer, Robert Stevenson, who had written in their defence that the lights of the Tay were quite adequate as they stood. When the Admiralty came out with the statement that the Tay was one of the best-lit rivers in Britain, the prospects for a lightship looked slim indeed.

Still the Harbour Trustees stuck to their guns and the confrontation became deeply personal at times, especially between powerful landowner and Trustee David

Hunter and Captain John Kennedy of Trinity House, who grew to loathe the sight of one another. In 1875, after lengthy negotiations, the Harbour Trust paid £15,000 to the Fraternity for lights, buoys and other equipment and also cleared a debt the latter had incurred to the Public Works Loan Commissioners. At long last they had gained control of the Tay buoyage.

The Trustees immediately formed a sub-committee to arrange for 'a good, staunch and substantial wood lightship' to be built. So keen were they on the idea that they made inquiries in London, Liverpool and Hull about the chances of acquiring a lightship on loan, to use until their own vessel was ready for sea. They were out of luck.

The lightship provoked much interest among the seafaring community and included in the correspondence dealt with by the sub-committee on the subject was a letter from a Master Seaman in Dundee, Captain A. Trail. Trail urged them to equip the lightship with steam-driven propelling machinery. It was a moment when history might have been made but Trail's letter suffered the ultimate fate – deferred for further consideration – and it was quietly forgotten about. Thus by a lack of will, or inclination, was the Tay denied the opportunity to introduce the world's first powered lightship. It was a very early example of the deafness that was to descend upon the lighthouse authorities of the British Isles whenever the subject was raised.

On January 17th, 1877, the contract to build the lightship was awarded to James Roney of Arbroath. He wasted no time and at the sub-committee meeting of February 3rd, he turned up with a beautifully constructed scale model of the lightship. Roney, who was obliged under the terms of the contract to deliver the completed article to Dundee within eight months, was a shipbuilder of the old school. He had learned his trade at the Alex Stephen yard on Marine Parade in Dundee, famous for the stout wooden ships they built for Dundee's huge whaling fleet and themselves destined to build a wooden lightship in 1889 to mark the North Carr rocks off Fife Ness. Much of the credit for the siting of the *North Carr* Lightship was due to a brewer, former Provost of Dundee and Northern Lights Commissioner, Hugh Ballingall.

Roney's yard at Arbroath cost him £120 a year to rent. His was a rash, even fool-hardy venture, the town's entire shipbuilding industry having collapsed four years previously. Roney's first order was for a 200-ton brigantine, the *Jane Rennie*, for a Mr Rennie of Arbroath. Roney built just five more ships before he was sunk by iron, his tiny operation driven under by the avalanche of competition from the builders of metal ships.

His second, the *Abertay* Lightship, easily outlasted the others possibly because of its exacting specifications. The *Abertay*, at 117 tons and just 90 feet long on the waterline, was small for a lightship due to occupy an anchorage exposed to the full fury of the North Sea. She was required to be built of wood which had been seasoned for at least 12 years. It turned out to be nearer 15. Much of the oak planking was half an inch thicker than required by her insurers, Lloyds. Her bottom was contracted to be covered in felt then sheathed in copper to prevent attack by shipworm, a marine bivalve mollusc with an insatiable taste for timber.

With typewriters yet to come into general use, Roney suggested in a handwritten note of fine copperplate style that he could trim £39 off the price by substituting what he described as 'yellow metal' for copper. He was referring to Muntz metal, a type of brass consisting of 40% zinc and 60% copper, invented in 1832 by George Frederick Muntz in Birmingham, the heart of the British brass industry. It was highly resistant to corrosion by salt water. The Trust would have none of it even though there was a minor risk of an adverse chemical reaction between the copper they insisted upon and the iron mooring chains. The *Abertay* was built for the full contract price of £3476.

A site had been selected for her in the mouth of the river with the Buddon Sands to the north and the Gaa Sands to the south. The Tentsmuir Point option had long since been discarded. The Trust were offered, and accepted for the sum of £167, a glass and copper lantern from the Elder Brethren of Trinity House, London, whose permission was required before any navigation light could be introduced anywhere off British and Irish coastlines. The light was to be carried 30 feet above deck on the foremast and consisted of nine oil lamps, each with its own silverized reflector, the whole to be rotated by the suspended weight 'grandfather clock' principle.

At their meeting of August 23rd, the Trustees agreed to invite the Master and Mate of the *Bar* Lightship, the main mark for shipping entering the Mersey for the port of Liverpool, to visit Dundee to instruct the crew of the *Abertay*. She was launched three weeks later, towed to King William Dock in Dundee and placed in the old graving dock.

The Harbour Trustees can hardly have failed to note with satisfaction that the barque *Alma* had gone ashore on the Elbow End in the river mouth on Friday, October 5th, laden with wooden battens for Grangemouth. Any lingering doubts about the need for a lightship there disappeared overnight. On the evening of October 11th, the ship's lantern was tested and found to perform satisfactorily.

The Courier & Argus of Saturday, October 13th, 1877, carried this Notice to Mariners on its front page:

> *The Trustees of the Harbour at Dundee hereby give notice that on or about the 15th of October, 1877, a LIGHT VESSEL will be moored near the entrance to the River Tay and opposite the Abertay Spit with the following bearings and distances, viz:-*
>
> *Two miles S.E. and a third North from Buddonness High Light Tower; 6½ miles E.S.E. of Tayport lights; and two miles N.W. and a third North from the Fairway Buoy; five cables lengths (about 1,050 metres) N.E. from the Elbow End; two cables W.N.W from No. 3 red buoy on the Gaa Sands. The lightship will ride in 5½ fathoms (10 metres) at low water. She will exhibit from her foremast from sunset to sunrise, a FLASHING WHITE LIGHT every 10 seconds, visible in clear weather about eight miles distant. During foggy weather a bell will be rung. The light vessel will have two masts and be painted red, with the word 'ABERTAY' in white letters on her side.*

A severe westerly gale plagued the middle days of the month, dying out on the evening of the 15th. The ship was moored the next morning, Captain Menzies commanding. He had been engaged at a remuneration of £2.10.0 per week, his Mate received £1.15.0 and his crew of three seamen £1.8.0. Each man went to sea bearing the gift from his employer of a single suit of working clothes.

The light was first exhibited on the bitterly cold evening of October 16th. There were some snow flurries but the light burned well and marked effectively the vital turning point in the channel through the sandbanks. The crew had a brand-new ship and a brand-new set of instructions to go with her. Most important of these was the emergency procedure for observing vessels in distress. For such incidents on the Buddon Sands side of the river, the lightship's signal gun was to be fired twice in close succession; rockets were to be fired and blue flares shown. On the Gaa Sands side, the gun fired once, also with flares and rockets, the process to be repeated every 15 minutes until acknowledged by the Buddonness High Light Tower.

Now that the ship was on station, if the light needed attention – for instance if any of the lamps blew out – a man had to climb the mast no matter the weather and attend to the problem. The main task of the crew (one was always ashore on leave), was the tending of the lantern. First duty of the day was the hand-winching of the lantern to the deck from its position round the mast and the cleaning of it, a chore that took about 2½ hours. The lantern weighed 17 cwt, equal to 864 kilograms, and was encased by day in a protective metal housing. Lamps and reflectors were taken below and placed in secure racks to await nightfall.

At regular intervals the wicks were trimmed. A hard crust would form as they burned and had to be broken off. A man would climb the rigging to two iron rail-ings circling the mast below the lantern. He would stand on the bottom rail, lean with his back against the higher one and with elbows wedged into the glass windows of the lantern, raise the glass chimney from each lamp and poke off the crust with a stick. It might take him half an hour, longer in bad weather.

In the generator room the other member of the two-man watch kept an eye on the clock which caused the light to revolve. This arrangement consisted of finely-balanced cogs propelled by a weight which dropped steadily to the floor and had to be rewound every 30 minutes. A bell warned that the weight was almost down.

The *Abertay's* daytime recognition mark at the top of the mast was a latticework ball six feet in diameter. A man could stand up inside it. The practice of showing daymarks was gradually phased out as the 20th century advanced until only the names were left to identify lightships by day. The old *Abertay*, however, retained her daymark until she came out of service. The two cwt fog bell on the foredeck soon became an off-station signal, its original function carried out by a steam-powered siren which could be heard in Dundee ten miles away grunting out its pattern of three blasts every 65 seconds. The tank providing steam held five tons of water, heated by a coal fire. The tank would often run dry and seawater had to be used, drawn at low tide when the water was at its freshest. It was necessary to keep testing the density of the water to see that the valves did not become clogged with salt deposits.

The *Abertay* shipped 100 two cwt bags of coal at a time, heaved on board using the lifeboat davits. Fresh water was pumped by hose from the relief tug into a tank which held six tons. The tank inevitably picked up extraneous material and when the level of fresh water became so low that it barely covered the bottom of the container – which happened often – the men were virtually drinking mud.

The tug called every two weeks, usually on a Wednesday, weather permitting. Among other stores it delivered the fresh food that had to be supplied by the families of the crew out of their wages. Meat was usually pre-cooked and sealed in fat to preserve it in the event of a relief being delayed. The tug also exchanged the crewman with the lugubrious look whose leave was at an end for the shore-bound shipmate with the satisfied grin.

Press reports at the time of the deployment described the living quarters as being 'airy and commodious'. However, in the shallow water the ship rolled so much that every single piece of furniture had to be screwed down. On the dining table a wooden frame kept plates and mugs from flying off and teapots and kettles had wire attachments which allowed them to be hung up at a moment's notice. Laying down a hot teapot in any kind of swell could be a painful mistake. Detachable wooden barriers fitted to bunks prevented the sleepers from being pitched out. Over the entire 62-year working life of the ship successive crews had good reason to curse the lack of bilge keels, which were usually fitted to lightships to help 'stiffen' their motion in heavy seas. Little wonder the men looked forward to their seven days ashore every five weeks.

The introduction of the lightship to the waters of the Tay was widely welcomed and during a lecture on lightships in the Independent Templar's Hall, Dundee, just four days after the *Abertay* moved into position, Mr Theodore Delport was frequently interrupted by bursts of applause. Mr Delport ventured the opinion that Britain had the best-lit coastline in the world.

At sea, the *Abertay* crew witnessed, on October 31st, the first of many whalers to pass them on their way to port. The *Narwhal* had spent six months hunting around the fringes of the Arctic ice and here she was, home with the products of seven whales from which about 85 tons of high-grade oil would be extracted. Out of touch as she had been, she must have been surprised to raise a bright-red lightship on her way into the river.

The *Abertay* had two 2-ton anchors always in the water, one to hold her on the ebb tide, the other on the flood. It was a system favoured where there was insufficient room for a lightship to swing to a single anchor. One anchor was customary in the lightship service, the ship able to move freely around it as she was shifted by wind and tide.

A major plus point of a lightship over a lighthouse and a major minus point may be summed up in the same word – movement. A lightship had the priceless flexibility to shift its ground if, say, a shoal began to alter its character and had to be marked at a different point. But unlike a lighthouse it could never be kept in exactly the same spot. Riding to a single anchor at the very end of a 500-metre cable, the ship in theory at least could change its position by 1,000 metres every six hours as the tide went in or out. In practice this did not happen that often but the space was needed to cater for that degree of movement.

The *Abertay* could not be given such leeway. She was in a tight area and her leash had to be kept tight too. Her anchors were placed a considerable distance apart, joined by a chain. To this chain on the seabed the main cable leading up to the ship was attached by means of a swivel. It was shorter than a single-anchor cable, restricting the ship's sideways movement as she drifted into position to ride to either upriver or downriver anchor. Once settled in position she would ride to a cable which encompassed both the chain leading down from the ship and that portion of the ground chain taking the strain of holding the ship. Riding to her downriver anchor, the cable ran to a maximum of 105 fathoms, to the upriver anchor, to 75 fathoms. An added safety factor permitted the ground chain to break at any point other than the swivel and leave the lightship still held by one anchor.

The *Abertay's* anchors were of the Martin type, first patented in 1867 by a Frenchman of that name. Two big flukes formed the 'hands' of the anchor's arms, which could move freely on a hinge at right angles to the main bar. Pulled from above, the anchor began to move, turning the flukes and driving them deep into the seabed. The power of the sea occasionally overcame even this mighty grip and the *Abertay* would get out of position. In this event the ship displayed two black ball shapes by day and at night exhibited the red off-station lights and rang the bell.

Dundee Harbour Trustees' delight with their new toy was such that they began to think about another one. At a meeting of their pilotage committee on December 8th, 1884, it was agreed to campaign for a new lightship to be moored 1½–2 miles outside the Fairway Buoy. Craftily, they decided to approach the Board of Trade to have this ship supplied and maintained as an Imperial Light, so absolving them of the expense of building and running it. The Board was not staffed by innocents however and they blew this impertinent suggestion clean out of the water in March, 1885, informing the committee that the Commissioners of Northern Lights would not be granted permission to spend any money on such a project, even if they wished it.

In the early spring of 1917, with a year of the First World War still to run, the *Abertay* was moved at the request of the Admiralty to the Blae Rock off Burntisland deep inside the River Forth and re-named *Outer Channel*. The Navy's suggestion that the Harbour Trustees might care to contribute towards the cost of maintaining the lightship while she remained in the service of the King drew the same frosty response they had themselves received from the Board of Trade 32 years before. The Trustees did grumpily agree to waive any hire charge for their ship. In her new place of employment the vessel had several narrow escapes from floating mines.

By the end of the war she was back on her old stamping ground, a trusty sentinel and friend to the craft which regularly plied their trade on the Tay. But a silent friend. Radio was now standard equipment on lightships although the sets were withdrawn during the war for security reasons. The *Abertay*, however, would have to continue to use a grossly inadequate semaphore signalling system until the summer of 1924 when she finally got a radio telephone link with the office of the Harbourmaster in Dundee. The equipment was installed by the Marconi Wireless Telegraph Co. Ltd., at a cost

The *Abertay* Lightship during one of her maintenance spells in dry dock in Dundee.
She was overhauled every three years.
Photograph courtesy of D.C. Thomson & Co. Limited.

of £1640. The set on board ship ran on an accumulator, charged nightly by a small petrol generator.

A veteran of countless gales, the *Abertay* left it late in her career before experiencing perhaps the worst of these. It all began on January 20th, 1937 in the form of a radio message requesting assistance from the Broughty Ferry lifeboat.

The weather was foul. An easterly gale had entangled the lightship's mooring chain with an underwater object, later identified as the wreck of the privately-owned steam tug *Protector*, registered in North Shields, which had been sunk in a collision in six fathoms of water two cables' lengths inside the lightship on August 29th, 1889. The snagged cable was giving the crew a very rough ride and the lifeboat, the *Mona*, stood by her all night until the weather moderated. But the worst was yet to come.

On Saturday morning, January 30th, another storm combined with a huge tide fell upon the luckless lightship. Her cable was still caught up and this time it parted, pushing the ship about 250 yards before she was checked. The *Mona* was again called upon and launched into a blizzard, this time to take off the crew. They weren't at all keen to leave their ship and it took a direct order from the Port of Dundee General Manager and Engineer, John Hannay Thomson, to persuade them to do so.

Dundee's Port Manager, J. Hannay Thomson. Photograph courtesy of D.C. Thomson & Co. Limited.

All round the east coast of Scotland the storm was causing chaos. In Kirkcaldy parts of the esplanade were under 12 feet of water. Waves were breaking against the doors of houses 50 yards beyond the sea wall. The residents were stunned by the fury of the assault from the sea. Part of the breakwater at Aberdeen harbour was smashed down, isolating the lighthouse on the end of it. Shore Street in Anstruther was under water. The rounded end of the cross pier at St Andrews harbour had been demolished and the Swilken Burn, part of which runs across the first and eighteenth fairways of the world-famous Old Course in the town, had changed direction.

In the turmoil of the Tay estuary the *Mona's* coxswain, Jim Coull, faced a major difficulty in extricating the crew from the lightship. It was barely possible to see 20 yards through snow being driven horizontally by the 70 mph easterly gale. Another dangerous complication concerned the lightship herself. Her boats, hanging in davits over the sides, were unguided missiles, thrashing about just waiting for a target like the lifeboat. By loud hailer Coull told the lightship crew to cut away their starboard boat, which crashed into the water and was obliterated from sight in a second by the blanket of white.

Edging up to the *Abertay*, Coull's men were able to throw aboard a grappling hook attached to a thick rope. The coxswain now manoeuvred his boat five times against the lightship, a man jumping onto the lifeboat each time. Assistant Master David Mearns was last to jump, clutching the ship's logbook. It was 2 pm.

Aboard the *Mona* as a volunteer was skipper of the *Abertay*, John Gall. Deeply vexed for his crew, which included his son David, Gall had been having the most miserable of shore leaves.

'It has been a perfect nightmare,' he said. 'We have had little sleep.'

One of the *Abertay* crew, Edward Lancaster, was landed at Tayport where he stayed. Lancaster was eventually to become Assistant Master of the lightship. When the remainder of the crew were put ashore at Broughty Ferry, they were met by cheering crowds. The men were unshaven, stiff and sore and gasping for a cigarette, their supplies having run out days before.

If they were now safely on dry land, other seafarers were in such peril from the off-station lightship that the port of Dundee had to be closed for the first time in its history. Effectively this had already occurred, the weather having deterred any vessel from attempting to cross the Tay bar for the previous 24 hours. But the *Abertay* had dragged her remaining anchor and was now straddling the channel. As if this were not bad enough, the light on the Fairway buoy had gone out and black buoys nos. 1, 2 and 3 were adrift and red buoy no. 4 was out of position. From Trinity House in London, general wireless calls were made conveying the message that the port was closed. Ships heading for Dundee began to alter course for other destinations along the east coast.

Hannay Thomson now directed all his considerable energies to getting his harbour open to traffic again. A specially-commissioned train was bringing a massive gas buoy from the Northern Lighthouse Board depot at Granton, Edinburgh to place upon the *Abertay's* correct position, but before the river could be declared safe for navigation the ship herself had to be moved somehow. With the weather in its present mood this was out of the question.

Seething with impatience, Hannay Thomson could do nothing but wait out the storm like his unattended lightship. The commercial life of Dundee Harbour was under unprecedented pressure. Storage sheds at Victoria Dock and Western Wharf were packed to the rafters with goods awaiting transport by sea. Nine ships were trapped in the port. One, the Currie Line trader *Gourland*, had an unusual cargo to say the least, consisting in part of three elephants and other circus animals bound for Hamburg. She had already made one attempt to get out of the river but in the narrow channel baulked at the prospect of squeezing past the gyrating lightship and returned to King George Wharf. Here it seemed likely the crew would be confronted by a difficulty not in the usual line of duty – coping with a trio of seasick elephants.

One of the harbour tugs had also been downriver to check on the lightship and reported that she was taking her punishment 'like a duck'.

Bailie Alexander Smith of Monifieth, convener of the Lighting and Buoying Committee, told the Harbour Trustees that the lightship had recently been over-hauled at a cost of nearly £900 and was expected to survive.

'Unfortunately,' he added, *'having no motive power she was at the mercy of the elements when she lost her moorings.'*

The tough old seamark *did* survive but not unscathed. When she was brought into port by the tug *Harecraig* on Tuesday, February 2nd, surveyors found that both bow and stern rails and her steering gear were damaged and that she had lost both lifeboats, one of which was recovered when it was washed up at Broughty Ferry. The compass and binnacle had disappeared overboard. The ship had no refrigerator and meat was stored in a safe kept on deck. That too was gone.

The *Abertay*, which lost her compass during the storm, here has her new compass checked by new Master David Mearns on March 27th, 1937. The ship's steering wheel was of practical use only when she was under tow.
Photograph courtesy of Mrs Catherine Simpson.

The ship herself was still seaworthy and after another refit and a trial run under tow, she was put back on station in late March. But her days were numbered. She was replaced in July, 1939 by a steel light vessel built at the Caledon Shipyard, Dundee. It had no engine. During the handover of her duties to the new ship, the old *Abertay* suddenly swung round and rammed the impertinent newcomer, damaging her own bowsprit. In the worldwide manner of seamen, those present scoffed at any prosaic explanation for this involving temporal elements like wind and tide.

The vessel was retained by her owners as a possible block ship for the duration of the 1939–45 war. She was scrapped at Woodhaven in 1945, a sad end for a ship whose history we now know includes a longer spell tugging at a chain than any other lightship in Scottish waters. What a gem she would be today as part of a collection of ships recalling Dundee's rich maritime heritage!

Still, she had proved a worthy, if unsteady monument to the craft practised by James Roney and his kind; men who worked as the scent of carpenter's glue hung heavy in the air, listening as they moved with a tuned, subconscious ear to the gentle rustle of wood shavings about their feet.

LIGHT BITES

The range of lightship lights continued to be included in some Notices to Mariners which accompanied the laying of a new light vessel, even though this was dangerously misleading. To say that the stated distances had to be taken with a pinch of salt may be an appropriate phrase. Much more than with lighthouses, lightship lanterns were subjected to salt spray which clouded the glass and reduced the range of the light. Even more significant in the days before the introduction of electric systems was the soot which gathered on the inside of the glass. Every lamplighter knew that when his squeaky-clean lantern was lit at dusk it carried far greater penetrating power than just before dawn.

Photograph courtesy of Mrs Catherine Simpson.

David Mearns joined the *Abertay* as a seaman in 1930. He won promotion to Assistant Master seven years later and became Master when the ship was returned to service after the storm of 1937. When the new *Abertay* began her career shortly before the outbreak of the Second World War, he was in charge. The war was just a few weeks old when an extraordinary situation presented itself.

Mearns was wakened by a crewman shaking him gently and whispering in his ear:
'Come topside skipper and take a look at this.'

Mearns was instantly aware of some unfamiliar noises. He dressed quickly and made his way to the deck, to find a German U-boat alongside his ship. The submariners were carrying out repairs to which they bent with a will, completely ignoring the lightship crew. Wisely, Mearns decided they would *not* ignore any radio message from the *Abertay* and he did not immediately report the incident which, as he drolly remarked, was in clear contravention of lightship regulations. The Germans remained alongside for hours, using the light vessel as cover for their activities, before slipping away in the dark.

Shortly afterwards the lightship was withdrawn to Dundee and Mearns applied to join the Royal Navy. He was told firmly that he would be looking after the *Abertay* instead and he was assigned to be her guardian at her berth in the Earl Grey Dock. So began for the skipper a strange and macabre term of duty. The region round the dock was a magnet for seamen from all over the world with its many pubs and the cheap food available at Hungry Mary's soup kitchen. The rigidly enforced black-out proved unsuited to this tide of often intoxicated humanity and Mearns was regularly roped in by the police to help them recover bodies from the water.

'At one stage,' he recalled, *'we were fishing them out of the dock at the rate of one every ten days or so. I could never get used to the fact that some of them still had their caps on.'*

The *Abertay* was moved again, to Woodhaven on the opposite side of the river, where she spent the rest of the war. Mearns and his old sidekick Edward Lancaster made a number of friends among the Norwegians who operated the Catalina flying boats based there.

Immediately the war ended the *Abertay* was requisitioned by the Admiralty. On May 9th, 1945, with Mearns in charge of an all-Navy crew, the ship was towed by the lighthouse tender *Pharos* to a point 45 miles off Montrose to mark Gap A, a channel which had been cleared through the coastal minefield and which was already being well used by ships from the Baltic and Scandinavia. Mearns took his pet dog along with him. The skipper could not have guessed that his acquaintance with the underwater wolves of Admiral Doenitz was about to be resumed. At Gap A, a U-boat surfaced and offered its surrender to the lightship. Mearns really ought to have sent it into Aberdeen, the nearest major port but he thought that Dundee, a submarine base during the war, deserved the glory. He radioed his base and sent it there.

Shortly after the conclusion in August of the *Abertay's* spell at Gap A, Mearns joined the Coastguard service and had stints at Anstruther and Blyth in Northumberland before taking up his final post at Carnoustie. David Mearns died in 1964.

The *Abertay* resumed her duties in the Tay estuary on February 4th, 1946. In the summer of 1971, at a cost of £120,000, she suffered the indignity of becoming the first light vessel in Europe to be fully automated and was painted a highly appropriate black to mark her new official designation of 'light float'. When replaced by a high focal plane buoy in the mid-December of 1984, she was towed to Harwich to serve as a test rig for the Trinity House automation programme and was eventually scrapped in the spring of 1992.

Lightships of the Yangtze River

*N*ot all floating lights were lightships or buoys. Some very odd craft played a vital if fleeting part in the development of coastal and river lights. In the United States, unattended beacon boats were employed in places like Delaware Bay in the late 18th century. They carried no light but did have distinctive daymarks on their masts.

Lightboats came later, tiny forerunners of America's lightships. They were moored in bays and rivers and were not manned. Bell boats also appeared briefly. These upgraded beacon boats carried a number of small bells as a fog warning, the action of the waves providing the motion to sound the bells.

In China, the lighting of coasts and rivers had until the latter half of the 19th century proceeded in a haphazard manner. The country's first modern coastal light – a lightship – was established in 1855 to mark the dangerous Tungsha Spit where the Yangtze River spews out into the Yellow Sea. A visit to the area in 1858 by the Scottish nobleman, the Earl of Elgin, revealed a much-improved situation. He wrote: 'A floating lighthouse (the lightship), a succession of buoys to mark the channel and a light tower apprised me as I entered the mouth of the Yangtze that I was approaching a port (Nanking) where trade was on a healthier footing than I had found in those times I had previously visited.'

A second lightship was laid further upriver to mark the Langshan Crossing in 1861. Other random improvements included the placing of a lantern upon the mast of a sunken ship – arguably classed as a lightship, if an unusually damp example. It was left to another Briton, Irish-born Sir Robert Hart, to organise a proper system of coastal lights and their long-term funding. Between 1863 and 1908 he was Inspector General of Chinese Maritime Customs. When Hart took up his duties, revenue from tonnage dues was just 8 million taels per annum.* Hart set about raising this revenue until by 1868, 27 million taels were being collected at a total of 32 ports. The Chinese Government was deeply impressed, especially since Hart's revenues were virtually the only dependable guarantee for loans negotiated by the Chinese, his department by common consent the only one in the endemically corrupt government to be run with probity and honesty.

In April, 1868 Hart established a new force, the Marine Department of Customs, headed by a Marine Commissioner under his own office of Inspector General. The new department was charged with providing and maintaining lighthouses, lightships, buoys and beacons; the removal of wrecks; improvement and conservation of channels into harbours; control of anchorages and the management of a skilled workforce to oversee all of these tasks.

Sir Robert divided the country's huge coastline into three districts, each with its own inspector, to whom local harbourmasters were answerable as were lightkeepers, harbour police and pilots. The northern section was based at Chefoo, the central at Shanghai and the southern at Foochow. When Hart first set up his Marine Department, there were in operation three lightships, six lighthouses and numerous buoys and daymarks. His first order of business was to create a systematic aids to navigation scheme marking the approaches to Shanghai, the centre for two thirds of all China's overseas trade. Next phase was to mark the Formosa Strait and the more dangerous reefs along the full sweep of the coastline.

By 1875, just seven years after the creation of the department, a chain of lights and other navigation aids led into every major harbour. The Yangtze River posed particular problems. China's major watercourse and one of the great rivers of the world, the Yangtze ran for 3000 miles – more than three times the length of Britain – sometimes changing its name as well as its course as it first raged then rambled its way from Tibet to the sea where its estuary was 60 miles across. The last 1700 miles of the river were navigable and bore about half the seaborne commerce of all China, not to mention the interchange of local produce between the provinces carried upon thousands of native sailing craft. Steamers of up to 6000 tons could reach as far as Hangkow except in the depths of winter. As a highway of communication and trade the river had no rival in any other part of the globe.

Making it safe for navigation was a matter of the deepest urgency. Part of the answer lay in another version of the lightboat, this one probably large enough to merit the term 'lightship'. At 50 to 60 feet in length, the Chinese craft compared in size to some of the lightships of the Humber and Mersey rivers in England. The *Whitton* on the Humber, for example, established in 1877 was just 40 feet long. The smallest lightship on the Mersey was the *Crosby*. Although no dimensions are available, it was smaller than the *Formby* which weighed a mere 81 tons and carried two more crew than the *Crosby*.

On the Yangtze, these red-painted vessels were placed at critical points. While many western world lightships were still conversions from other types, those on the Yangtze were built especially to do the job by Chinese carpenters. The craftsmen used a junk design except for the bow and stern, both of which were pointed to enable the craft to ride to anchor in all conditions. They had no means of movement and were towed into position. At night they displayed red or white lights or a combination of red and white in either horizontal or vertical array. Each carried a black spherical daymark. Deckhouses were painted white.

During the late 19th century 47 such vessels were anchored along the lower Yangtze. This astounding number, added to the coastal light vessels, dwarfed the lightship fleets of every other country except Britain, which in 1865 had 51 lightships and was probably a close second to China at that time. The Americans were in third place with 39.

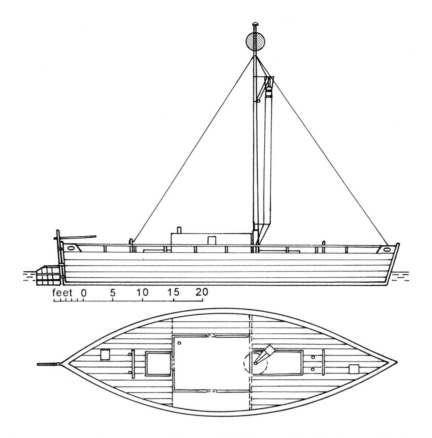

Plans showing the general arrangement of the wood-built Yangtze River lightboats or lightships.
Length would be 50 to 60 feet, with an 18 to 20 feet beam.
Courtesy of the United States Lighthouse Society.

Unlike the much earlier American lightboat, the Chinese equivalent was manned. The three seamen assigned to each one were engaged in a chancy profession. The constant stream of traffic sweeping by posed a high risk from collision and in winter, ice floes presented another danger. These hazards paled into insignificance, however, compared to that posed by the juggernauts of the Yangtze. Rafts of timber, supposedly under the control of one or more ships, regularly plied the river. Up to 100 metres in length they were difficult to manage and sometimes broke loose. Thundering downriver, they swept all before them.

Instructions to lightship crews if they saw one of these rafts bearing down on them were to slip their mooring and buoy the end of the mooring before fleeing. What often happened in practice was that the raft fouled the buoy and broke the mooring, at the same time taking over and destroying the vessel and drowning its crew. In the faster-flowing middle Yangtze, these lightships proved too frail to survive and bigger, steel ships were employed. Eventually all the wooden lightships were replaced by steel-hulled craft.

Sir Robert Hart's contribution to the seaborne trade of China and the safe passage of ships entering or leaving the country can hardly be overstated. His organisation of the lights and buoys of that gigantic, heavily-populated nation raised the number of employees of his department from 200 in 1864 to 5704 by 1901. Sir Robert came to be so highly regarded by the Chinese Government that he was often consulted on a whole range of issues unconnected with his department and he handled them all with a deftness of touch that deserted him just once. He was convinced that the rebels of the anti-foreigners Boxer uprising of 1900, whatever else they did, would spare his own house near Peking. Well thought of he may have been, but the Boxers burned his house to the ground, destroying many irreplaceable records which included his personal diary covering his entire service in the Orient.

Sir Robert was, not unnaturally, assisted by British technology during his 48-year mission as the keeper of China's lights. The English firm Chance Brothers provided most of the lenses for the country's lighthouses and lightships. But it was Sir Robert himself who provided a spectacular example of how the foresight and drive of a single individual could be directly responsible for the saving of countless lives both during and well beyond his own lifespan.

When he retired in July, 1907 and returned to Europe in the following January, it was just his fourth trip home since 1865. He died in 1911, the bearer of dozens of awards and honours from his own country, including a baronetcy, and from a grateful Chinese nation.

*Although the Chinese were almost certainly the first people to employ coins as an element of currency, the Chinese Custom House tael was not a coin but a unit of weight used to measure pure silver. The value varied with the price of silver. Value of a tael in 1905 was reckoned at three shillings and one tenth of a penny. Transferred at this value to 1868, Sir Robert's tonnage dues income at that time gives a notional worth of just over £4 million sterling.

LIGHT BITES

The final fragment of Sweden's 130-year-lightship history (1844-1972), lies anchored off the Wasa Museum, Stockholm. Built in 1903 at the Gefle Works, *LV 25* was substantially redesigned in 1927. Her steam-powered propulsion unit was replaced by a powerful 403 hp Bolinder motor to drive the ship through the ice that plagued the Gulf of Bothnia for much of the year. An ice-breaking bow was also fitted. The ship spent most of her working life on one of the two Finngrundet stations. She can still deliver her old lighting sequence of two consecutive flashes every 20 seconds.

When the *Girdler* Lightship was rammed and sunk in the Thames estuary at midnight on Friday, June 20th, 1884, the crew were taken off by the other vessel, a passenger liner, and landed at Dover. The offending ship, reportedly with about 400 passengers on board, resumed its voyage to Sydney, Australia. The report on the incident by Lloyds agent at Whitstable claimed that the ship which rammed the *Girdler* was the P & O steamship *Indus*. P & O were not amused for the *Indus* at the time of the collision was berthed at London's Royal Albert Docks. 13 days after the accident the lightship was raised and taken inshore for repair.

The English lightship *LV 13* proved an unlucky number for telephone cables. On November 12th in 1961, while on the East Goodwin station, she broke adrift and her emergency anchor fouled the St Margaret's Bay/La Panne No. 6 GPO telephone cable. Before the lightship was taken in tow by the T.H.V. *Vestal*, the spare anchor and cable were left in the water at the request of the GPO. When the *Vestal* recovered the ship's original cable, also pulled up was an old anchor and 90 fathoms of cable, plus an aircraft propeller. On December 29th, 1965, the ship again went adrift, this time from the Outer Gabbard station and ended up four miles out of position. The *Vestal* was again called in to reposition the ship and while grappling for the anchor, found it entangled with an old telephone cable. The ship, retired in 1990, was bought by a Captain Hoffman, who converted her into a floating restaurant and pub at Stade, Germany. She was moved in 1993 to her current berth in City Sporthaven, Hamburg.

Bibliography and Source Notes

1.   *Looming Lights,* George Goldsmith Carter
2.   *Keepers of the Lights,* Hans Christian Adamson
3.   *Danish North Sea Lightships,* Morten Hahn-Pedersen
4.   *The Modern Book of Lighthouses,* W.H. McCormick
5.   *Ladies of the Lakes II,* James Clary
6.   *The North Carr Lightship,* Paula Martin
7.   *The Glasgow Herald,* February 14th, 1914 and May 25th, 1914
8.   *The New Yorker,* June 2nd, 1934
9.   *Standing Into Danger,* Andrew Jeffrey
10. *The Times,* November 3rd, 1789
11. *The People's Journal,* February 6th, 1937
12. *The People's Journal,* July 15th, 1939
13. *Strong to Save,* Ray and Sussanah Kipling
14. *Keepers of the Sea,* Richard Woodman
15. *The Keeper's Log* (US Lighthouse Society magazine, Spring 1994)
16. *Aalloilla keinuvat majakat,* Seppo Laurell
17. *Brake Light Vessel – a Story of Two Collisions,* Anthony Lane, from Bygone Kent, volume 14, no.6, June, 1993, page 327.
18. *The Manned Lightships of the Humber,* Captain D.C. Thomas
19. *The Lightships of the Flemish Sandbanks,* J.C. Pohrel and C. Harbion
20. *Off Station,* Nick Lambert
21. *Usque ad Mare. A History of the Canadian Coast Guard and Marine Services,* Thomas E. Appleton. Source: Fisheries and Oceans Canada, Canadian Coast Guard. Data reproduced with the permission of the Minister of Public Works and Government Services Canada, 1997.
22. *The San Francisco Chronicle,* June 15th, 16th and 17th, 1916
23. *Sentinels of the Sea,* Ronald R. Burke
24. *Southern Lights – Lighthouses of South Africa,* Harold Williams
25. *A History of Modern Norway,* 1814-1972, T.K. Derry
26. *Sweden – Historical and Statistical Handbook,* volume 2, 1916
27. *A History of Sierra Leone,* Christopher Fyfe, 1962
28. *The Bell Rock Lighthouse,* Robert Stevenson
29. *The Morning Chronicle,* Halifax, Nova Scotia, May 25th, 1914
30. *The Times,* June 24th, 1884
31. *Aberdeen Journal,* March 28th, 1899
32. *Disaster at the South Goodwin,* Anthony Lane, from Bygone Kent, volume 13, no.1, January, 1992, page 2.
33. *Wooden Light Vessels,* Anthony Lane, from Leading Lights, volume one, no.2, 1995.

LV 15 (Channel) under tow in a gale in the English Channel. The Channel was the last manned lightship station in British waters. Photograph by the Rt. Hon. Lord Greenaway, Younger Brother of Trinity House.

Other sources:

International Association of Lighthouse Authorities list of members, June 1992

Report to the Humber Conservancy Board on the Lighthouses, Lightships, Light Floats, Buoys and Vessels belonging to the Board, A.E. Butterfield

The Annual Report of the Maritime Museum of Finland, 1989-90

Head Department of Navigation and Oceanography, St. Petersburg, Russia

Information Department, Trinity House, London

The Guildhall Library, London

The Northern Lighthouse Board, Edinburgh

The University Library, St Andrews

United States Lighthouse Service Instructions to Employees (1915)

Local Studies Library, Paisley

The John Oxley Library, Brisbane, Australia

The National Maritime Museum, Darling Harbour, Sydney, Australia

US House of Representatives Document No. 22, 1870–*Wreck of Scotland* Lightship

Shore Village Museum, Rockland, Maine, Newletter Number 1–93 March 31st, 1993

The Lighthouse Digest, June 1994, Vol III no. 6

Leading Lights, Volume I, no. 9

Kjell Loyland, Kystverket, Oslo

Dundee City Archives

Thanks for individual help and contributions are due to: Zoe Madans; George Rosie; Tom Henderson; W.H. Pulfer; John Gillies; Peter Wintgen; Edward Bourke; Mrs. G. Payne; Harold Pitchers; Jan Jaap Kruk; Tricia Burke; Joyce Symington; William Pomeroy; Geoff White; Kathy Brown, Editor, *The Light Keeper*; Arthur Tillett, Research Officer, Queensland Maritime Museum; Dennis Conroy, Senior Administrative Officer, Australian Maritime Safety Authority; David Gray; Anne-Grete Erikssen; Peter Williams; Geoff Tully, Hon. Secretary, Ramsgate Branch, R.N.L.I.; David Bedlow, Commissioners of Irish Lights; Mrs Catherine Simpson; Mr Gordon Wise, Dover Coastguard.